You Can Live in Jesus' Easy Yoke:
With His Rhythms of Grace for your Daily Stress

By Bill Gaultiere, Ph.D
© 2010

SoulShepherding.org
949.262.3699
Bill@SoulShepherding.org

How *Easy Yoke* Came to Be

There's an old saying, "When a student is ready the teacher appears." I am first and foremost Jesus' student, his apprentice.

One of the greatest blessings of my life was meeting Dallas Willard in 2003. I was at the beginning of a great spiritual renewal – I was a ready student. Dallas quickly became my "key mentor," the one God uses to unlock treasure stores of "the knowledge of the glory of God in face of Christ" (2 Corinthians 4:6). His influence is all over this book.

I am thankful for the many people like you that God has sent me who, along with me, are ready students in Jesus' school of discipleship. Since 2006 I have been speaking and writing on *You Can Live in Jesus' Easy Yoke* to pastors and lay people alike, in churches, homes, and classrooms and on the Internet – they have brought out in me the teacher, or rather the assistant to the Teacher.

I am particularly thankful for the pastors and ministry leaders at the Crystal Cathedral who in 2010 joined me in apprentice groups using *Easy Yoke*, and then led groups for others: Chuck, James, Jim, Paul, and Rocky in our men's group and Debbie L, Debbie T, Jan, Louise, Marge, and Sara in our women's group.

Easy Yoke would have remained a series of lessons that got e-mailed to people if it weren't my friend Karen Porter. God uses her to do amazing things to bring out the writer in people and to get that writing out to vast audiences. You can contact Karen at kaeporter@gmail.com or by phone at 281-797-3920.

You Can Live in Jesus' Easy Yoke:
With His Rhythms of Grace for your Daily Stress
By Bill Gaultiere, Ph.D

"Make yourself stand out" (Perfectionism Survey) $\Rightarrow$
"Draw people to Jesus"
Bless your Competitors
For other people I pray, "In Christ's humility consider others better than yourself"

You Can Live in Jesus' Easy Yoke: Introduction
Come to Jesus

I've been a Christian for over 40 years now. But I haven't always lived as an apprentice[1] to Jesus. In many ways I have wanted to keep my feet in two worlds: God's kingdom and my kingdom.

But in the year 2002, the year before I turned 40, the Lord got a hold of my heart in a new and deeper way.[2] I realized that I had lost the passion for Christ that I had as a young

---

[1] "Apprentice" is a term that Dallas Willard uses for disciple. Sadly, our understanding today of discipleship to Jesus is quite watered down from the one that 1st Century followers of Christ had. Thinking in terms of being an apprentice to Jesus makes our discipleship concrete and practical; it emphasizes that we learn from being with Jesus and working side-by-side with him over a long period of time.

Today we think that to be a disciple of Jesus is optional and that it's for Christians who are really serious. It used to be that to be a "Christian" was to be a disciple of Jesus. In fact, in the New Testament the word "Christian" is only used three times and the word "disciple" is used 269 times. The New Testament was written by disciples of Jesus, for disciples of Jesus, about discipleship to Jesus. All the promises of the New Testament are for disciples of Jesus. If you're a "Christian" but not apprenticing yourself to Jesus then the blessings God wants to give you won't readily flow your way. (See "Discipleship: For Super Christians Only" by Dallas Willard in his books *The Spirit of the Disciplines* (Harper: 1988), p. 258-265 and *The Great Omission* (Harper: 2006, p. 3-12.)

[2] I was participating with Kristi in "The Journey of Desire," which was a weekend conference led by John Eldredge. I am so thankful to God for John's ministry of "Ransomed Heart" that got me back on the life-giving way of Christ.

adult. *I prayed earnestly for Jesus to be my First Love again.* I had to rekindle the fire and spread it to others!

So I returned to reading the old classics of Christian devotion that I had loved as a young adult. I resumed being more diligent to practice disciplines like fasting, silence and solitude, and memorization of Scripture. I met regularly with Ray Ortlund for spiritual mentoring and prayer over a number of years.[3] I became a student of Dallas Willard – reading and re-reading all of his books and listening over and over to his classes on spiritual formation – and met with him for personal guidance and prayer.[4]

I wanted to learn from Jesus how to live my *whole life* in God's kingdom. I re-submitted and re-dedicated my life to Christ. I wanted to live by Ray Ortlund's heart-throbbing

---

[3] I consider Ray Ortlund the father of my spiritual renewal and the inspiration behind the *Soul Shepherding* ministry to pastors and leaders that I lead with my wife Kristi. "Be Devoted to Christ Like Ray Ortlund" is my article on SoulShepherding.org that highlights the key transformational lessons that rubbed off on me from my years of soul talk, Bible study, and prayer with Ray.

[4] Much of the material presented in this course comes from what I have learned about following Jesus from Dallas Willard, especially the over 2,000 hours I have spent listening to his classes on CD. He told me, "You don't need to quote me. If what I say is any good it didn't come from me anyway – it came from Jesus." Nonetheless, along the way, when it seems important I will direct you to some of Dallas' books. "An Author Mentor Becomes a Soul Friend: Reflections on Dallas Willard's Ministry to Me" is my article on SoulShepherding.org about some of the key lessons that I have gleaned from my conversations with Dallas.

prayer: "Be all and only for Jesus!"[5] I wanted to work for Jesus and no one else.

It was a decision. And a prayer of devotion to Jesus that I call "The Apprentice Prayer." Most every morning for eight years now I have been offering this prayer from my heart (in words more or less like these):

> Jesus, I love you! Father, I adore you. Holy Spirit, I rely on you.
>
> Lord Jesus, I seek to live as your apprentice in all that I do today. I relinquish my agenda for this day and I submit myself to you and your kingdom. In all things today I pray, "Your will, your way, your time."
>
> Dear Father, I ask you to ordain the events of this day and use them to make me more like Jesus. You are sovereign and I trust you that you won't let anything happen to my family or me today, *except that it passes through your loving hands.* So no matter what problems, hardships, or injustices I face today help me not to worry or get frustrated, but instead to relax in the yoke of your providence. Yes, today I will rejoice because I am in your eternal kingdom, you love me, and you are teaching me!

---

[5] Ray Ortlund's book, *Lord, Make My Life a Miracle!* (Regal Books: 1974), is filled with his enthusiastic insights on living for Christ, loving one another, and reaching the world with the Gospel.

My Lord, I devote my whole self to you. *I want to be all and only for you, Jesus!* Today, I love you with all my heart (intentions and choices), all my soul (personality), all my mind (thoughts and feelings), all my strength (body and energy), and all my relationships (conversations and interactions).

Today, I depend on you, Holy Spirit, not my own resources. Help me to keep in step with you.

Today, I look to love others as you love me, dear God, blessing everyone I meet, even those who mistreat me.

Today, I'm ready to lead people to follow you, Jesus.

Amen.

Years later, by the grace of God, I remain enthusiastic about being a devoted apprentice to Jesus!

Some people think I'm crazy. One day I got an e-mail from one of the thousands of readers of the *Christian Soul Care Devotional* that I send out by e-mail.[6] She wrote:

"I like the way you want us to 'delight' in the Lord like a 'child,' as I've always felt this is the way God would love us to approach him. But I don't know if I would 'skip' like a child and then say, '*I am the*

---

[6] You can view some of my past bi-monthly devotionals and sign up to receive future ones at SoulShepherding.org.

disciple Jesus loves.' I think my roommate just might call the 'men in the white coats' on me!"

I replied: "Bring on the white coats! I'll be crazy for Jesus!"

This is Your Chance!
Jesus is standing before *you* right now as you read these words. He's smiling and his arms are open to you. *His heart is open to you.* "Come to me," he says. "Follow me and I will give you life – real life, my life in God, abundant and eternal living, more vitality than you could imagine, more joy than you can contain, the peace that you've always longed for."[7]

If only we would let Jesus ravish our hearts! If only we would appreciate the glorious blessing of being a part of his kingdom of the heavens in our midst. If only we would see that awaiting us right now is the opportunity of a lifetime: to be Jesus' beloved disciple, to make our lives Jesus' classroom, to make our world his kingdom, to shine his light all around us.

When we behold in our hearts the goodness and beauty of Jesus, then we will be captivated by him! We will leave behind anything that distracts us and lay down all the burdens that we're carrying in order to take his hand and walk with him wherever he leads. And in the pages of the New Testament we see person after person doing *whatever* was required to get to Jesus and the life he offered.

---

[7] These are my words based on John 10:10 and similar statements Jesus made.

People shouted out at the top of their lungs and made fools of themselves to get Jesus' attention. They pushed their way through crowds or crawled in the dirt and between people's legs to touch him. They walked across deserts, sat in the hot sun for hours and hours, and skipped meals to listen to him teach. They left their businesses and their families to follow him. They endured ridicule and abuse to be his disciples. They jumped out of trees, ripped the roofs off houses, and gave up their life savings to fall at his feet and worship him!

What are *you* ready to do to come to Jesus? How about joining with some friends to apprentice yourself to Jesus in an eight-week long group training experience?

You Can Live in Jesus' Easy Yoke is a course that aims to *ravish your heart with the Lord Jesus Christ and his kingdom of love.* Each week you will be invited to come to Jesus and participate in his "life that is truly life" (1 Timothy 6:19). We'll learn how to live as Jesus' apprentice in his easy yoke and thereby be set free from anxiety, stress, hidden hurts, self-criticism, hurried living, over-working, eggshell walking, and jealousy.

My message to you is that it is possible for *you* over time to grow to the point that you *easily and routinely* walk in the character and power of Christ, consistently enjoying his peace (no matter how bad your circumstances are) and shining his light to the people around you (no matter how difficult they are). You don't need to be a "super Christian" to become more like Jesus – it's open to anyone. You simply need to devote yourself to being his *apprentice,* seeking to learn from him little-by-little how to do all that you do with him *in a world in which transfigurations still happen.*

This Easy Yoke Gospel may seem too good to be true for you. At first it did for me too. But I discovered that this *Life* is not just for Jesus. David, Mary, John, Paul, and many other Biblical characters grew in God's abundant life. I personally am growing in Christ's life and have been blessed to pass it on to others in psychotherapy or spiritual mentoring – and then to see them pass it on to still more people. Let me share our stories with you with the hope that this will inspire you to grow in Jesus' easy yoke and to share your story with others.

So with the Apostle Paul, in the humility of a wounded healer, I want to say to you in these pages: "Follow me as I follow Christ" (1 Corinthians 11:1, paraphrase).

Triangle of Soul Transformation[8]
How can you become more like Jesus? What is your part to grow in God's grace? Each chapter in *Easy Yoke* is based on the understanding that to be spiritually formed in the

---

[8] I have been using "The Triangle of Soul Transformation" for a number of years. I adapted it from Dallas Willard's "Golden Triangle of Spiritual Growth," which focuses on (1) The Action of the Holy Spirit, (2) Ordinary Events of Life: Temptations, (3) Planned Discipline to Put on a New Heart, all centered in the mind of Christ (See *Divine Conspiracy*, p. 347). I also incorporated Dallas' three-step model of change from *Renovation of the Heart*: (1) Vision (2) Intention (3) Means. My triangle is similar to the one James Bryan Smith uses (also adapted from Dallas) in *The Good and Beautiful God* (Intervarsity Press: 2009), p. 24: (1) Adopting the Narratives of Jesus, (2) Engaging in Soul-Training Exercises, (3) Participating in Community, all centered in the Holy Spirit.

image of Christ there are three fundamental ways that we need to respond to God's gracious initiative in our lives; three ways that by coming to Jesus with others we can be transfigured more and more into his glorious image. God is continually at work in our lives by his Word and Spirit, but it's up to us to participate in what he's doing:

Believe Jesus' Gospel.
Each chapter will present a deceitful and damaging cultural assumption held by most people, like, "If at first you don't succeed, try, try, and try again!" We will then show how Jesus' Gospel of the kingdom of God ("Re-think your strategy for life because God's Kingdom is open to you now," paraphrase of Matthew 4:17) counters that message and invites us to live in his easy yoke that transforms us.[9]

Studying and meditating on the Bible, especially the Gospels, is essential for our spiritual formation. We all have been "conformed to the pattern of this world" and by God's mercy need to "be transformed by the renewing of our minds" in Scripture (Romans 12:1-2). It is singularly *the life of Jesus Christ,* and learning to participate in his life by his Spirit of grace, that unleashes the goodness and power of Bible to renew our minds. So each chapter will look at an important aspect of Jesus' character and his easy yoke training that for us that comes out of who he is.

---

[9] James Bryan Smith's book *The Good and Beautiful God,* and the others in his "Apprentice Series" does a great job of helping us to identify false narratives that are undermining our trust in Jesus' gospel of the kingdom.

Practice Spiritual Disciplines.

Spiritual disciplines work by indirection: they are activities that *we can do* that with God's help enable us to do what *we cannot do.*[10] To grow spiritually we need to try different ways of interacting with God's grace and applying his Gospel to our lives. We need to rely on Jesus as our Spiritual Formation Coach, asking him to guide us in using the practices that are best suited to transform us in the ways that we need it most. We do this *experimentally,* adjusting what we do and how we do it based on what is most helpful for our healing and growth.

Jesus introduces three general types of spiritual disciplines in the Sermon on the Mount: giving/service, prayer/Scripture, and fasting/self-denial (Matthew 6:1-18). In *Easy Yoke* we will use spiritual practices from all three categories because they work together to renovate our whole person: heart, soul, mind, strength, and relationships.[11]

Each chapter will introduce you to a new spiritual discipline aimed at a specific need for soul transformation.

---

[10] This is Dallas Willard's definition. *The Spirit of the Disciplines* (Harper: 1988) is his book that goes into depth about how to practice spiritual disciplines for transformation in Christlikeness.

[11] Using Jesus' Greatest Commandment as the model (Mark 12:30-31), Dallas Willard identified these parts of a person: heart (spirit or will), mind (including thoughts and feelings), body, relationships, and soul. He explains that each part of your self needs to be understood and it needs to interact with God's grace-giving Word and Spirit for healing and growth so that your whole person can be transformed to be more like Jesus. He summarizes this in his "Circle Diagram" in *Renovation of the Heart* (Navpress, 2002) p. 38.

The discipline will require that you make a space (self-denial) to engage with God and others through praying Scripture and sharing honestly on how your relationship with God is going. To help you apply that discipline in your daily life we will work with a Bible-based "Breath Prayer."[12] Additionally, you will be encouraged to serve others with your listening, encouragement, and prayers.

Learn from Daily Life Trials.
Each chapter will focus on a particular stress-related problem that many people struggle with. You will be challenged to *find God and his kingdom in the middle of your difficulty.* In other words, stress is an *opportunity* to learn that Jesus' easy yoke is present for you even in the midst of your hurts and troubles.

You Can Live in Jesus' Easy Yoke is designed for use as part of a small group or spiritual friendship. Each of us needs to be part of a community of apprentices to Jesus in order to become more like him. So for each chapter to help you

---

[12] A Breath Prayer is a way of Abiding in Prayer that goes back to the Desert Fathers of the 3rd and 4th Centuries. There are a variety of ways you can use Breath Prayers, but the basic idea of how I do this is quite simple: you meditate quietly and deeply on a selected verse (or paraphrased verse) of Scripture. To help you to slow down your mind, calm your body, and center your thoughts on Scripture you breathe the words of the prayer in and out. Whenever your mind wanders you gently bring it back to the short prayer. You're seeking for the Word of God to descend from your mind down into your heart, which is your *will* (where you make choices and decisions and orient your life).

With practice using Breath Prayers can become a delightful habit of the heart that facilitates healing and growth in Christlikeness.

Read my articles "Abiding in Prayer" and "Breath Prayers" on my website, SoulShepherding.org to learn more.

assimilate what you are learning from Christ you'll be encouraged to use the "Salty Questions" to share and pray with your spiritual friend or group.

Triangle of Soul Transformation
God's Word and the Holy Spirit minister to us in community and we respond to...

Believe Jesus' Gospel
Replace your false personal narratives with Jesus' Gospel: "Re-think your strategy for life because God's Kingdom is open to you now." Submit to the Lord and follow him in all things.
(Matthew 4:17)

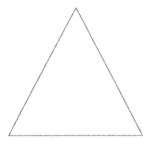

Practice Spiritual Disciplines
Use praying Scripture, self-denial, and service experimentally to train with Jesus as his disciple, applying his Gospel to your life and learning to obey him from your heart.
(Matthew 6:1-18, 2 Timothy

Learn from Daily Life Trials
Accept your difficulties as tests of your character growth. As personal weaknesses are uncovered share these with spiritual friends who help you to rely more on Christ.
(John 16:33, James 1:2-6)

The three corners of this Triangle of Soul Transformation (above) work together. You can't fully do one without also doing the other two as each feeds into the others. Generally the flow of change is A-B-C (but it also goes in other directions). For instance, to really learn from Jesus in the Bible we need to make application to our lives through spiritual disciplines. The effect of our spiritual disciplines on making us more like Jesus shows up in real life situations, especially our difficulties and relationships. And as go through trials we often see that we need to go back to Jesus and the Scriptures to re-think on a deeper level about how we're living our lives.

A Final Word About Commitment
To benefit from *You Can Live in Jesus' Easy Yoke* you need to make four commitments:

- Attend a 90 minute weekly meeting to learn, share, and pray with four to six other apprentices to Jesus. (You can also do your meetings in a triad or with one soul friend.)
- Participate in the meetings by being honest with group members, staying on topic, keeping confidential the personal things that are shared, listening to others without giving advice, and praying for the people in your group.
- Prepare for each weekly meeting by devoting about two hours to read the material, study the Bible passages, experiment with the spiritual exercises, and respond to the "salty questions" (seeking Christ in your challenges and struggles).
- Practice being Christ's Ambassador to the people in your life contexts, shining your light in ways that invite others to follow Christ with you.

Imagine I am part of your group and we are having conversation: we talk about what we're learning, share personal stories of what God is doing in our lives, try out some spiritual disciplines and report to one another on the experience, and pray together about things we're struggling with, encouraging one another to find God in the middle of our stress.

How *Easy Yoke* Came to Be
This curriculum was birthed as an attempt to consolidate a number of years of teaching on the easy yoke of Jesus and offer it for a large number of people at the Crystal Cathedral. We started in summer of 2010 with a group of pastors and leaders that I've been blessed to work with: Chuck, James, Jim, Paul, and Rocky in our men's group and Debbie L, Debbie T, Jan, Louise, Marge, and Sara in our women's group.

Now these Crystal Cathedral leaders are leading groups or classes with other apprentices to Jesus. Also, ministry leaders that I work with in other settings are using this material to mentor apprentices to Jesus, namely my dear friends and co-laborers in the vineyard, Fatu and Margaret. And there will be others. *Welcome to each one of you!*

In September 2010 I completed a second version of *You Can Live in Jesus' Easy Yoke.* This is a work in progress. Please share with me your experience.

Thank you for following Christ with me on this adventure!
Bill
Bill Gaultiere, Ph.D., Co-Founder, Psychologist, & Spiritual Director
Soul Shepherding, 4000 Barranca Parkway, Suite 250, Irvine, CA 92604
949.262.3699 ~ SoulShepherding.org ~ Bill@SoulShepherding.org

You Can Live in Jesus' Easy Yoke: Lesson #1
Step into the Easy Yoke of Jesus

In 2009 I won a medal for finishing the "Surf City" marathon in Huntington Beach, CA. I ran 26.2 miles in under 4 hours. It was actually the 5th marathon that I've completed and it was my slowest one, but it might be the one I'm the most proud of because I did it at 46 years old. The other four I did in the physical prime of my life, between ages 17 and 21.

You're probably thinking to yourself: "I couldn't run 26.2 miles!" Or maybe, *"I wouldn't want to run 26.2 miles – it'd be too hard!"*

Try Harder!
Most people think that to be successful in anything they need to *try really hard.* Most of my life I've thought that way. We say to one another and to ourselves things like…
"If at first you don't succeed, try, try, and try again."
"It's up to me to make it happen."
"I have to take control of the situation."
"I need to get a grip on my emotions."
"Life is hard."
"I can do better if I just try harder."

Are these true statements? Is this God's wisdom for you and I to live by? In life, is God urging us: "C'mon. Try harder!"? No. They may be half true, but ultimately they are false belief systems.

Imagine trying to finish a marathon just by trying hard! Picture yourself determined to run 26.2 miles without stopping or even walking – even though you haven't even run one mile in years. But you're motivated! You're going to run hard! You're going to push yourself to keep running no matter how tired and sore you get!

Your body and my body won't let us run long distances without building up to it over time. It doesn't matter how much will power we exert. If we try to force ourselves to run farther or faster than our capacity then we'll run out of breath or be in too much pain to continue. And if we somehow keep making ourselves run anyway then eventually we'll start throwing up, get injured, or collapse in exhaustion.

There is no doubt that effort is required to run a marathon, but it is not sufficient. The spiritual life works the same way. You can't sustain godly behavior by telling yourself that you must do what you should. You know this is true because, like me, you've tried to do what you should! You've told yourself things like, "Be kind... Don't get stressed... Don't get angry about that... I need to pray more..." You've tried and *tried harder* to do what you should and sometimes you've succeeded (which usually leads to pride) but then eventually you weren't able to sustain your good behavior – discouraged, you may have given up trying altogether.

The religious Scribes and Pharisees in Jesus' day tried hard to do what they should. Theirs was a legalistic righteousness that was depressing, destructive, and deadly. Jesus called them "whitewashed tombstones" – on the outside they were clean, manicured, and surrounded by flowers, but inside they were full or rotting flesh and dead bones (Matthew 23:27-28, paraphrased). Jesus said that our righteousness must go far beyond theirs (be a totally different kind!) if we want to enter the kingdom of God (Matthew 5:20).

Do you Have A-N-X-I-E-T-Y?

The "try harder" mentality leads to anxiety. Let's see how you're doing with anxiety. Try my screening test to identify any symptoms of A-N-X-I-E-T-Y that you may struggle with. Each of the seven categories of anxious symptoms has two or more related questions. Underline the questions that you answer with yes, meaning, "That's mostly true of me."

A gitated. Are you easily frustrated? Do people irritate or upset you? Do you lose your temper often?

N ot sleeping/relaxing. Are you having trouble getting to sleep or staying asleep? Do you often wake up and not feel rested? Is it hard for you to be still and relax?

X fears. Do you have any fears that you accommodate by avoiding situations? Are you afraid of social situations, interpersonal conflict, rejection, failure, public speaking, leaving home, airplanes, spiders, knives, etc.?

I n your body. Have you been experiencing shortness of breath, heart palpitations, tightness in your chest, discomfort in your stomach or bowels, headaches, twitching, shaking hands, sweaty palms, or tingling?

E scalating worries. Are you worried about problems you're facing? Do you keep thinking over and over about your stress? Do your thoughts race out of control?

T raumas relived. Does your mind keep re-experiencing an upsetting event(s)? Are you having nightmares?

Y es all the time. Do you feel pressured to say yes to accommodate other people? Satisfy your perfectionism? Give in to desires that won't go away?

If you have yes responses in three or more of the seven categories (or any yes answers that are especially disruptive for you) that suggests that anxiety is shutting you off from God's peace, draining your energy, diminishing your effectiveness, and distracting you from opportunities to love God and the people around you.

Jen's Quivering Lip

Jen sought my help when she couldn't get her lip to stop quivering with anxiety when she talked. This embarrassed her socially and it became a problem for her in her job because as the Women's Ministries Director in her church she often had to speak in front of audiences. She knew that she was anxious about her lip and what people were thinking about her, *but she didn't know that she had a problem with trying to control things.*

In everything she did Jen tried hard. She wore the latest fashions and got her hair professionally styled every few weeks. She prided herself in making healthy meals for her family and being involved in her kids' lives. And after she put her kids to bed she stayed up late preparing the weekly Bible Study for working mothers which she led in her church.

Sometimes Jen's husband got frustrated with her that she didn't relax more and didn't have more time to go to shows, take bike rides to the beach, and do the things that they had enjoyed before having kids. But she always reassured him that things would get better when the kids were older.

Everyone who looked at Jen's life, including Jen, thought she had the perfect life. But Jen's quivering lip wouldn't stop. She found herself tightening her lips to try to get them to stop trembling. She was losing her smile! And she was becoming more and more self-conscious and anxious about the talks she gave at church and the small group she led in her home.

The harder Jen tried to keep up her ideal, put together image, the more she became anxious. She was frustrated with herself that she couldn't get her lip to stop quivering. And she was always afraid that people would notice her "flaw" and think less of her. So she kept trying harder to look good, prepare the best talks, be a great mother, and keep a lid on her fears and frustrations.

The more Jen tried to control her lip, the more it quivered. The more she tried to control what people thought about her, pressuring herself to do everything right and to look good, the more anxious she became.

Anxiety is a Control Problem
You may not have Jen's same symptoms of anxiety, but probably there are times that you have internalized stress and experienced anxiousness in one-way or another. I have and most people I know have.

How do we overcome our anxiety? How do we stop taking on too much stress and get free of the accumulated tensions in our body and soul? Advice from psychologists like me abounds. Some of it is helpful, but a lot of it just entices us to chase after a life of greater ease and happiness. This is *running toward a mirage!* Peace and joy are not obtained by trying to get them – they are *natural fruits of living the kind of life that is rooted in God's love.*

Centuries before the modern science of psychology was invented Francis de Sales[13] (1567-1622), a Jesuit priest and spiritual director, helped ordinary people struggling with anxiety and many other common problems. He appealed for them to set their hearts on God in the midst of their distress and learn to love the Lord Jesus Christ with all their heart, soul, mind, and strength. This wise soul doctor knew that devotion to the Lord is the source of heavenly peace!

If anyone strives to be delivered from his troubles out of... self-love... he will grow hot and eager in seeking relief, as though all depended more upon himself than upon God... Then if he does not find what he wants at once, he becomes exceedingly impatient and troubled, which does not mend matters, but on the contrary makes them worse, and so he gets into an unreasonable state of anxiety and distress, till he begins to fancy that there is no cure for his trouble...

This unresting anxiety is the greatest evil that can happen to a soul, sin only excepted. Just as internal commotions and seditions ruin a commonwealth, and make it incapable of resisting its foreign enemies, so if your heart be disturbed and anxious, it loses power to retain such graces

---

[13] As the Protestant Reformation was in full force, Francis de Sales brought reform *within* the Catholic Church.

as it has, as well as strength to resist the temptations of the Evil One...

Anxiety arises from an unregulated desire to be delivered from any pressing [problem], or to obtain some hoped-for good... Birds that are captured in nets and snares become inextricably entangled therein, because they flutter and struggle so much. Therefore, when you urgently desire to be delivered from any [problem], or to attain some good thing, strive above all else to keep a calm, restful spirit; steady your judgment and will, and then go quietly and easily [out of your snare]...

When you are conscious that you are growing anxious, commend yourself to God, and resolve steadfastly not to take any steps whatever to obtain the result you desire, until your disturbed state of mind is altogether quieted... so as to act rather from reason than impulse.

If you can lay your anxiety before your spiritual guide, or at least before some trusty and devout friend, you may be sure that you will find great solace. The heart finds relief in telling its troubles to another.[14]

De Sales is saying that anxiety arises from trying to control situations (the try harder script) in order to get what you want. Why do we worry about making things turn out a certain way? Because we don't like how we feel on the inside. We don't like being vulnerable or needy and we don't want to feel hurt, condemned, scared, or angry so we deny the unpleasant emotion and focus on improving

---

[14] Frances de Sales, *An Introduction to the Devout Life,* p. 202-204.

our external situation, believing that will make us feel better. But any relief we might experience is temporary. And all of our pressured activity just leaves us like that fluttering bird, trapped and tangled up in a net of anxiety!

One Word for Jesus
Some time ago I was meeting with Dallas Willard and in the course of our conversation he asked me, "If you had one word to describe Jesus what would it be?"

How would *you* answer that question? Close your eyes for a moment and consider this. Then write down the first words that come to mind. If you could only use *one word* to describe Jesus what would it be?

Have you stopped reading so you can give your own answer?! Go ahead take a moment *now....*

Jesus is *the* Word of all words! His is the name above all names. He is so magnificent and multi-faceted how could we pin Him down to just one word! And yet, I found this to be a very meaningful exercise. The words we pick and the ones we don't pick may have something to say about our relationship with Him.

Here are the words I thought of... Jesus is... Love... Compassion... Holy... Lord... Teacher... Risen... Healer... (These are *all* good words to describe Jesus.)

Then Dallas looked into my eyes and shared with me his word. You need to know that this was a special moment for me. He's my key mentor. I've read every book he's written more than once. I've listened (many times) to every audio teaching series of his I can find. In the last six years he has discipled me to Jesus in ways that have impacted all that I am and everything that I do as a Christian, husband, father, friend, psychologist, pastor to pastors, spiritual writer.

What One Word would Dallas Willard use to describe Jesus? "Relaxed."

Relaxed?

I would have never thought of that word! But ever since that conversation I haven't been able to stop thinking about Jesus being relaxed.

Think about it. Jesus had far and away the most important and dangerous mission that any human being has ever had or ever will have. And he had to wait eighteen years to begin working on it and then he had just three years (of public ministry) to fulfill it. And yet Jesus was *relaxed!*

Jesus needed to convince a large number people that although he was a human being like them he was also the unique Son of God. And his followers needed to be so confident in him as their Lord and Savior that they would give up their lives to lead other people to know him – even to the point of torture and death. And yet Jesus was *relaxed!*

Jesus could only be in one location at a time. And when he left one city to go to another he left behind people that hadn't been healed or discipled (Matthew 13:58). Most people – even his own family at first – rejected him and his message (Luke 4:28-30, Mark 3:20, 31-34). Many of the people he discipled deserted him (John 6:66). And even his faithful disciples didn't understand who he was until later when he would rise from the dead (Mark 8:31-33)! And yet Jesus was *relaxed!*

All his life long Jesus served people for the Father's sake and yet most of the time these people opposed him. He had no rest from being stressed by Satan, demons, wicked kings, contemptuous Pharisees, wealthy snobs, raging mobs, seductive prostitutes, flattering sycophants, party animals, and fickle friends. And yet Jesus was *relaxed!*

Jesus was tempted to sin in all the same ways that we were: arrogance, contempt, lust, greed, deceit, self-reliance, ambition, sloth, you name it and he could've done it and he was in situations that seemed to call for sinful responses (Hebrews 2:18). And he experienced all of our weaknesses and felt all the same painful emotions we feel like disappointment, sadness, grief, anger, fear, anguish, stress, anxiety, anguish, pain, and being overwhelmed (Hebrews 4:15, 5:2). He even felt guilt and shame because he carried our sin (2 Corinthians 5:21). And yet Jesus was *relaxed!*

The fate of all humankind – past, present, and future – depended on Jesus successfully completing his gospel mission! And yet Jesus was *relaxed!*

Jesus was crucified on a cross – tortured by enemies, abandoned by friends, insulted by passers by. *And yet Jesus was relaxed!*

When I have big responsibilities I sometimes start taking charge to make things happen. When I have lots to do I tend to hurry. When I am stressed by situations anxious feelings may control me. When I am criticized or rejected I might react by feeling bad about myself or getting angry. When I am in terrible pain I have difficulty being loving to others.

How did Jesus remain at peace when he was under pressures much, much harder than I face? He practiced what he preached! He lived in the same easy yoke that He offers to us. We need to think of Jesus as *the first disciple:* he apprenticed himself to the Father as a child and throughout his life, learning to live out the things he would later teach.

It's important for us to ponder deeply the mysterious reality that our sinless Lord "grew" (Luke 2:52); he "learned" (Hebrews 5:8) how to:
Maintain moment-by-moment submission to God's will, never saying or doing anything except as the Father directed Him (John 6:38, 12:50)
Pray without ceasing (John 11:42, 1 Thessalonians 5:17)
Be so dependent upon the Holy Spirit as to be filled with his presence and power without limit (John 3:34)
Bless those that cursed him (Luke 22:34)

Being relaxed in his Abba Father's arms of love – even when stressed, in pain, or being mistreated by enemies – is what enabled Jesus to love and to fulfill *all* the lofty words that we use to describe him.

Relaxing in Jesus' Easy Yoke
For most of my life if you had one word to describe me you would never have used the word "relaxed!" "Intense," yes! "Stressed," probably. "Anxious," maybe. Perhaps it's because my name – "Will I Am" – means "Determined!"

In my past when I had big responsibilities I would always try hard and then *try harder.* When I was stressed by situations I'd feel overwhelmed or anxious. When I had problems I worried. When I was challenged I tried hard to *make* things turn out right. When people looked at me I tried to show them my ideal self. I always pressured myself to do what was good.

Back then I thought that the Christian life was hard. Many Christ-followers think that. But that's only because we haven't learned to live in Jesus' easy yoke. In other words, it's not God who is making life so hard, but us! Paul promised us, "It is for freedom that Christ has set us free... Do not let yourselves be burdened by a yoke of slavery" (Galatians 5:1). The Apostle knew that following the risen Christ is not only the better life – it's also the *easier life!*

Eight years ago I opened my heart anew to Jesus and I began to appreciate Jesus' Easy Yoke Gospel that sets us free from the destructive "try harder" false narratives. (Recall that this is at the top of our Triangle of Soul Transformation.) I realized that with a smile and open arms Jesus was saying to me *personally:*

No one knows the Son except the Father, and no one knows the Father except the Son and those to whom the Son chooses to reveal him.

Come to me, all you who are weary and burdened, and I will give you rest. Take my yoke upon you and learn from me, for I am gentle and humble in heart, and you will find rest for your souls. For my yoke is easy and my burden is light (Matthew 11:27-30).

Do you know what a "yoke" is? It's a heavy wooden harness that fits over the shoulders of oxen. It is used in farming to attach two oxen together, neck to neck, and hitch up them up to a plow that they are to pull across a field to prepare it for planting. Jesus is saying that we are all like oxen in that we have a yoke to wear in life. And the people that Jesus was talking to were in a yoke that choked them and they were carrying a burden that crushed them: they were yoked to the Pharisees and burdened by their legalism.

The Pharisees and religion scholars had tremendous power over the common people and imposed on them a religious system of keeping endless rules and traditions that came across as: "You're not good enough! Try harder! Do more! Do it better!" Jesus repeatedly confronted the religious leaders for their hypocrisy that kept them and the people they influenced outside of the kingdom of God. At one point Matthew records that Jesus pronounced seven woes on the Pharisees for their legalistic approach to relationship with God. For instance, Jesus said: "Woe to you, teachers of the law and Pharisees, you hypocrites! You clean the outside of the cup and dish, but inside you are full of greed and self-indulgence. Blind Pharisee! First clean the inside of the cup and dish, and then the outside also will be clean" (Matthew 23:25-26).

Wise farmers are careful not to pair a young ox with a poorly trained ox. On their own, young oxen might be strong and energetic, but they don't know how to wear the yoke around their necks and they don't know how to pull the plow: they jerk and strain to try to get out of the yoke. They charge forward to rush to the end of the job, chaffing their necks and choking themselves! Or they try to wander off to graze lazily in a meadow.

But if you take a young ox and pair it with an ox who has been well-trained then the mature ox shows the younger one how to wear the yoke *loosely and lightly* and how to pull the plow *slow and steady*, step-by-step, straight ahead. Then before long the field has been plowed and the oxen aren't bruised by the yoke or worn out from pulling the plow.

Jesus is like the mature ox that knows how to wear the yoke and do the work of plowing gracefully. He rejoiced to live as the Father's disciple in all that he did. *His righteous life, miracles, and wise teaching flowed naturally – graciously and effortlessly – out of his connection with his Father.* When he offers us his easy yoke he is inviting us into his way of intimacy with the Father. Let's re-read Jesus' grace-invitation to us in the poetic paraphrasing and inspired insights of Eugene Peterson in *The Message*:

The Father has given me all these things to do and say. This is a unique Father-Son operation, coming out of Father and Son intimacies and knowledge. No one knows the Son the way the Father does, nor the Father the way the Son does. But I'm not keeping it to myself; I'm ready to go over it line by line with anyone willing to listen.

Are you tired? Worn out? Burned out on religion? Come to me. Get away with me and you'll recover your life. I'll show you how to take a real rest. Walk with me and work with me – watch how I do it. Learn the unforced rhythms of grace. I won't lay anything heavy or ill-fitting on you. Keep company with me and you'll learn to live freely and lightly (Matthew 11:27-30, MSG).

Ahh! Yes! By coming to Jesus we can take a *real rest!* We can live in the *unforced rhythms of grace!* We can *live freely and lightly!* We can relax and enjoy our life and our work with God. And as God helps us to recover our life in Christ then we are empowered to love the people that we come in contact with.

Grace is Not Passive
Let's be sure we understand these "unforced rhythms of grace." We can't push our way to God, but neither can we be *passive* about it.

Tragically, in order to stay clear of legalism many Christians today end up being *paralyzed by grace.*[15] We think all we need to do is to go to church and have good doctrine or read the Bible and say our prayers. But doing just these standard activities, as we typically understand them, does not reliably transform people to be more like Jesus Christ. This is obvious when we look at the character of the average "Christian" in America. The Holy Spirit does not *zap* people into Christ-likeness through inspiring sermons! God does not leap off the pages of the Bible and *make* people into loving disciples of Jesus!

Commonly we say that grace is "unmerited favor." But that doesn't tell us where grace is how it relates to our life

---

[15] Dallas Willard writes, "Currently we are not only saved by grace; we are paralyzed by it." *The Great Omission: Reclaiming Jesus' Essential Teachings on Discipleship* (Harper: 2006), p. 166. If you haven't read any of Dallas' books yet this is a good one to start with.

today. We tend to limit God's grace to our need for forgiveness of our sins so we can go to heaven when we die. But grace is so much more than that – it is for all of life!

Grace is God acting in our lives generously and powerfully to do what we cannot do on our own. God acts and we respond. God's hand reaches out to us and we take hold. The Lord leads us and we follow him. It's up to us to *interact with* and *rely upon* God's favor and mercy in all that we do. Just as much as its true that, "Apart from Jesus you can do nothing" (John 15:5, paraphrase) so also its true that, "If you do nothing it will be apart from Jesus."

We need to understand that grace is not opposed to effort; it's opposed to earning. Earning is an *attitude* of pride and self-sufficiency, but effort has to do with taking appropriate *action.* Jesus teaches us that in order to get into his easy yoke we need to act – we have to respond to his loving initiative in our present circumstances – or we'll miss out on the rest of soul that he offers us.

Our Lord says to us in the easy yoke passage of Scripture:

- Be "willing to listen"
- "Come to me and get away with me"
- "Walk with me and work with me"
- "Watch how I do it"
- "Learn"
- "Keep company with me"[16]

---

[16] These Matthew 11:28-30 phrases are from the NIV, *The Message,* or my own paraphrases.

Again and again in the Gospels Jesus taught us *not to try to make things happen for ourselves,* but to follow his lead in all that we do:

Anyone who intends to come with me has to let me lead. You're not in the driver's seat; I am. Don't run from suffering; embrace it. Follow me and I'll show you how. Self-help is no help at all. Self-sacrifice is the way, my way, to saving yourself, your true self. What good would it do to get everything you want and lose you, the real you? What could you ever trade your soul for? (Mark 8:34, MSG; see also Matthew 16:24 and Luke 9:23).

Being active in God's grace seems like a contradiction to us, but its not. Peter summarizes this way of getting into Jesus' easy yoke and following his lead in all that we do by telling us to "Grow in the grace and knowledge of our Lord and Savior Jesus Christ" (2 Peter 3:18). And similarly the writer to Hebrews teaches us to "Make every effort to enter [God's] rest" (Hebrews 4:11).

Instead of trying harder and pushing to make things happen for ourselves we can learn to put our effort into relying on *Christ with us,* listening to him, and following his lead step-by-step. This is the Good News Gospel! This is the truth we can know through interacting with the grace of Christ and thereby be set free (John 8:32) from the burdensome cycle of trying hard... Feeling guilty (or proud)... Trying harder... Getting exhausted and discouraged...

Don't Try, Train[17]

Running the marathon was actually relatively *easy* for me (except for the last six miles!) because I didn't just try – I *trained*. I became a marathon runner *on the inside* – in my body and my mindset – so that in the race I could show myself to be a marathoner on the outside.

Every Saturday morning for months before the race I did a long run. I started with a four-mile run that goes alongside the two lakes near my home. Then each week I went a little farther, building up to a 20 mile-long run in the hills. I also did other running and worked out with weights. I really should've trained more than I did, but I prepared enough to enable me to finish the marathon with a decent time.

The secret to my workouts and to any training program is *indirection.* You can't improve or grow directly, just by trying hard. Instead you do what you can do at that point in time and with repetition over time you are eventually able to do what you could not do at the start. By disciplining yourself to practice your exercises you get stronger and better and are able to do more with less strain.

It's because of my training that I was able to enjoy running the 26.2-mile race. What a thrill it was to run on paths lined with people cheering me on as I made my way through parks and along the ocean. And then what a joy it

---

[17] In *The Spirit of the Disciplines* Dallas Willard teaches that the key to transformation in Christ-likeness is practicing spiritual disciplines in order to live in the easy yoke of Jesus.

was to cross the finish line with thousands of people —
including my wife and three teenagers — cheering for me!

What I enjoyed most about my marathon was the time to
be quiet, meditate on Scripture, and to pray. That's why I
run. *I run with Jesus.* He is the Champion of Psalm 19 who
is rejoicing to run his course in the heavens all around me
(verse 5). So as I run I fix my eyes on Jesus. I converse with
him. I follow him. He is the author and perfecter of my
faith (Hebrews 12:2).

To grow spiritually, overcome anxiety, or learn in any area
of life we need to approach it like I approached my
marathon: *Don't just try, train!* The Apostle Paul was
apparently a fan of the Olympic games and he used this
analogy to teach us the disciples of Jesus need to discipline
themselves to grow in the grace of Christ:

Do you not know that in a race all the runners run, but
only one gets the prize? Run in such a way as to get the
prize.

Everyone who competes in the games goes into strict
training. They do it to get a crown that will not last; but we
do it to get a crown that will last forever. Therefore I do
not run like a man running aimlessly; I do not fight like a
man beating the air. No, I beat my body and make it my
slave so that after I have preached to others, I myself will
not be disqualified for the prize (1 Corinthians 9:24-27).

Train yourself to be godly (1 Timothy 4:7).

And Paul rejoiced to discipline himself spiritually! "Rejoice
always! Again I say rejoice!" was the refrain of his life with

Christ – even in the midst of painful trials and hard labors (Philippians 4:4). In Paul's spiritual life he ran for Christ like Olympic runner Eric Liddell was depicted in the movie "Chariots of Fire." As he sprinted around the track he was holding Scripture on a piece of paper, his head was tilted back as he was looking up to heaven, his arms flailed exuberantly, his mouth hung open wide with laughter, and he said to himself and to the world: *"God made me for a purpose. He made me fast! And when I run I feel his pleasure!"*

O dear friends, let's approach our life with Christ like Eric Liddell ran! We begin by asking the Lord Jesus Christ to be our Life Coach. We do spiritual "work outs" with him. He helps us to grow in his grace and become stronger in love by designing a training routine that is specially suited for our individual needs, issues, and personality. He guides us and encourages as we do our spiritual exercises. Then when we leave the gym he accompanies us. After all, he lives inside us! And actually, daily life is the best place to learn from Jesus. Our Mentor teaches and trains us in all that we do each day so that we can learn to do what we're doing in his easy yoke, relaxed in his love, free of anxiety.

The Kiss of Peace
Jen learned to bring her quivering lip and her anxiety to Jesus, the Wonderful Counselor and Prince of Peace. She stopped trying to control her anxious lip and instead got re-trained in how she dealt with her anxious feelings.

For starters she admitted to me that she had anxious feelings! We talked about situation after situation in her life and ministry in which *under the surface* she was afraid or worried. She talked with me about her fears of what people thought about her and the pressures she put on herself to be a successful pastor, wife, and mother and to keep her anxious emotions under raps. She learned to stop trying so hard to do better in everything she did and to start relying on God's unconditional love for her.

One of the most important things that helped Jen with her anxiety was learning to abandon to God the outcomes of whether or not her lip quivered, what people thought about how she looked, and the effects her presentations and group lessons had on people. Instead of trying to control these things she sought for the peace of Christ to rule her heart (Colossians 3:15).

What a blessing! Learning to walk in the easy yoke of Jesus was the *kiss of peace* for Jen that over time calmed down her quivering lip. Now and again it still quivered, but she hardly noticed because she didn't worry so much about her image – she was more secure in God's love for her.

Spiritual Exercise:
Abandon Outcomes to God

To become more like Jesus we need to apply his Gospel to our daily life, using spiritual disciplines as "means of grace"[18] that help us learn to become the kind of person who easily and routinely walks in the character and power of Christ. Recall that this is part of our "Triangle of Soul Transformation." A fundamental spiritual discipline for us to experiment with is submission to God.

Submission to God in all that we do is *the way* into the anxiety-free yoke of Jesus. In fact, there is *no other way* into Jesus' yoke. (Remember it is a yoke!) By living in submission to God, the Scriptures, and other people Jesus shows us that humility leads to true peace, power, freedom, and love for others. Richard Foster says that submission is "the ability to lay down the terrible burden of always needing to get our own way... If we could only see that most things in life are not major issues, then we could hold them lightly... In submission we are at last free to value other people."[19]

Jesus Lived in Submission

Perhaps the most astonishing aspect of Jesus' life on earth is that as the Sovereign Lord he lived by the discipline of submission! On every page of the Gospels we see Jesus

---

[18] Richard Foster writes in *Celebration of Discipline* (Harper & Row: 1978), his classic book, "By themselves the Spiritual Disciplines can do nothing; they can only get us to the place where something can be done. They are God's means of grace" (p. 6).

[19] *Celebration of Discipline* by Richard Foster, p. 97-98.

resisting temptations to make things happen for himself or to get people to think or do what he wanted. Instead he submits to the Father; he abandons outcomes to God.

Jesus Christ is the Lord God, co-equal with the Father and the Spirit in the Trinity, and yet he chose to live his life on earth in submission to God in all things, at all times. And this brought him great joy and peace and power!

Frank Laubach, a great evangelical missionary to Muslims and spiritual writer of the 20th Century, noted that the Apostle John indicates in his gospel that Jesus was acting "under God's orders" 47 times! John records Jesus saying things like: "I have come down from heaven not to do my will but to do the will of him who sent me… Whatever I say is just what the Father has told me to say (John 6:38, 12:50).

Jesus is the Word who spoke the Scriptures into existence and yet he lived in submission to those very Scriptures! Again and again we read in the gospels that Jesus said and did certain things "so that the Scripture would be fulfilled."[20] He discovered his identity, lived out his life story, and made his every decision according to the Scriptures.

At times in his life on earth the King of kings and Lord of lords even submitted himself to the people he created! Jesus confined himself to human flesh, was born in a stable and laid in an animal feeding trough, obeyed his parents, completed carpentry jobs for customers,

---

[20] Matthew 26:54, Mark 14:49, Luke 4:21, John 17:12, 19:24, 19:28, 19:36.

submitted to John's baptism, paid taxes, performed menial servant duties, relied on his disciples for support, surrendered to soldiers, subjected himself to illegal trials, yielded to Pilate's verdict, capitulated to the cross, and handed over his mission to his disciples.

If Jesus Christ, our Lord and Savior, lived in submission to God in all things then how could we do anything less?

How to Abandon Outcomes to God

Dallas Willard teaches that we can cultivate submission to the Lord as the demeanor of our heart by practicing the discipline of "abandoning outcomes to God."[21] This concept makes submission to God *concrete* so we can apply it to our daily life stresses. It has helped me, and many people like Jen that I've talked with, to get into Jesus' easy yoke and grow in his peace.

Everyday there are things that we want, situations in our relationships, work, ministry, projects, etc. that we'd like to have turn out a certain way, which, of course, is natural. But pushing for a certain outcome is not necessary and it is contrary to Jesus' easy yoke. It's helpful to identify a situation to practice denying yourself what you want in order to submit to God's sovereign leading. Instead of trying to make things happen the way you want in that circumstance you *let go* of your agenda and entrust the results to God.

"Let go and let God" is a good saying *if* it means, "Submit to Christ and follow his leading." But it is often

---

[21] See *Renovation of the Heart* by Dallas Willard.

misunderstood to encourage a "laissez faire" attitude of passivity and disinterest along the lines of, "It doesn't really matter and there is nothing I can do." But abandoning outcomes to God is not passive; it is an *active process* of anticipating situations, praying about them, being patient and attentive to God in them, and being responsible to do what needs to be done *while putting confidence in God to direct the outcomes.*

There are many ways to experiment with learning to abandon outcomes to God in your daily life. To make our submission to God practical it's helpful if we submit to a person as unto Christ. As John says in his epistle, "How can you love your unseen God if you don't love your brother or sister right in front of your eyes?" (1 John 4:20, paraphrased). When you practice abandoning an outcome to God, the key is your attitude of being in submission to Christ and his kingdom, drawing your peace and strength from the Lord in your midst.

Think about your life and the kind of situations that you worry about or try to make things happen. Then in anticipation of the days ahead pick *one or two* situations like these below to practice abandoning outcomes to God:

Wait and Pray Before Acting.
When you have an opportunity wait before pursuing it. Or in a situation that you need to give leadership pause before you act. First, pray along these lines: "Lord, your will, your way, your time." You might ask for guidance from a friend or a mentor. Be open to God re-directing you and giving you joy in his presence even if you "miss out" on what you wanted to do or say.

Prepare for Possible Disappointment.
With a project that you're working on consider the
possibility that you may not succeed or certain people may
not be pleased. Pray that God would help you to leave the
results in his hands. Of course, do your best, but don't
base your self-identity and self-esteem on how things turn
out. Determine to be satisfied and secure in God's
unconditional acceptance of you. Appreciate that what is
most important is that God uses all situations to form you
more into the image of Christ.

Be Genuine.
In conversation be careful not to present your ideal self to
impress people. Be honest and try sharing a weakness or a
personal struggle. (Or maybe you need to do the *opposite*
to learn not to put yourself down as way of eliciting
sympathy. In that case, be honest and try sharing a
personal strength or accomplishment with someone.)

Let People Cut in Front of You.
When you're driving let people cut in front of you and pray
for them as they do. Let go of your position or space on
the road. Remind yourself that you're not just in your car,
but you're with Jesus in God's kingdom and that's
wonderful!

Listen to Others First.
In a meeting let others speak first and promote the good in
their ideas. If you don't get to promote your agenda don't
worry about it. God is enough for you!

Don't be Defensive.
When someone misunderstands you or criticizes you don't
be defensive. Listen to their feelings, empathize, and

entrust your reputation to God. If you don't get to share your feelings and be understood relax in your Heavenly Father's arms of love.

As you take a situation like one of these and work on abandoning outcomes to God remember: Don't just try, *train!* We practice spiritual disciplines as means of grace, as ways to interact with God's generous favor so that we start changing on the inside. Think of a spiritual exercise as a way to "watch and pray" with Jesus *before* you get into the stressful situation. Spend some time in prayer anticipating the scenario that tempts you to try hard to make things happen or to become frustrated and anxious. Imagine yourself in that situation and pray that the Lord would help you to be relaxed in his easy yoke, to find peace in his caring presence with you and wait on him to see what he is doing.

A Breath Prayer of Submission to God
On the Cross Jesus let go of everything and abandoned all outcomes to the Father. To help him do this he prayed a line from Psalm 31:5 to his Abba: "Father, into your hands I commit my spirit" (Luke 23:46).

This is a most helpful prayer of self-denial and submission to God. We can apply it to any situation that we are stressed about or wanting to control. Simply identify the challenge, relationship, or other source of possible anxiety and pray: "Father, into your hands I commit _____."

Spend a few minutes using this little prayer to watch and pray with Jesus in order to become the kind of person who in that situation will abandon outcomes to the Father who loves you.

Perhaps try breathing the words of Jesus in and out, slowly and deeply. (This takes practice, but it is well worth the effort because it brings deep relaxation to your body and soul and it helps your mind and heart to absorb the Scripture you're praying.) Breathe in deep... Hold your breath... Exhale... Breathe in: "Father..." Hold onto the word "Father" and Spirit of Christ with your breath... Breathe out: "Into your hands I commit _____."

Or meditate on Jesus' words as you imagine him on the cross, giving his life out of love for you and all people. He's in the most horrific, painful trial, but he's drawing strength from his Abba Father. He's turned loose of everything – his dignity, his reputation, his comfort, his body, his very life – and he expresses his total abandonment to God in his prayer: "Father... into your hands I commit my spirit."

Then as often as you can throughout the day pause to breathe and shoot up a little arrow prayer[22]: "Father, into

---

[22] Ray Ortlund taught me to "shoot up little arrow prayers" to God as I went about my day. He said it's the key to life of peace and power. Brother Lawrence (1611-1691) called this "Practicing God's Presence." Here's how Ray illustrated this in *Lord, Make My Life a Miracle* (p. 27-28):

> Well, just begin right where you are. Inwardly begin to adore God. Begin to praise Him at the very depths of your being. Right now just say, "Lord, I love You. I praise You. I adore You! I want to live in your presence."
>
> Tomorrow morning when you get up, say, "Lord, here we are. What are we going to do today? I want to be with You all day long."
>
> "Fairer than morning,
> Lovelier than daylight;

your hands I commit _____ ." Make a fun game of it and see how many times you can remind yourself to offer up this prayer! This will help you to submit yourself to God and his kingdom as you do what you're doing and that in turn will help you to be ruled by the peace of Christ (Colossians 3:15).

Salty Questions

Reflect and pray on these questions. You may want to write your responses down in your journal. Be prepared to share *personally* with your group how the easy yoke teaching of Jesus is affecting the way you're dealing with your stress. Recall from our "Spiritual Formation Triangle" that accepting our difficulties as learning opportunities is one of the most important things we can do for our spiritual growth.

Dawns the sweet consciousness –
I am with Thee!"

Then all day long, behind the scenes, at the very deepest level, hold conversation with God. As you walk down the street, ask God's blessing on those you see.

As you stop at a stop light, express your love to Jesus.

As you go into your own home, "Dear God, today will You bless this home – and me, as I go in."

And as you go from here to there, "Praise to God. Thy will be done."

Keep the conversation running. It will take no extra time, my friend. It will take all your time.

And when you fail? ...Well don't spend lots of time groveling over it. Get up and go on. Go to God, and get on with Him again (p. 27-28).

Sharing honestly and praying earnestly for one another along these lines is being *salty for God* – it preserves what you've learned, adds God-flavor, and elicits thirst for more of God.

What is one thing you learned about how you can live your daily life in Jesus' easy yoke?

What is a recent example in which you struggled with trying hard too hard to accomplish something, controlling a situation, or were anxious?

How did it go for you this week with abandoning an outcome to the Lord to get into his easy yoke? How did breathing Jesus' prayer of submission to the Father help?

You Can Live in Jesus' Easy Yoke: Lesson #2
Smile in your Storm

Two years ago Kristi and I helped to lead a spiritual pilgrimage to Israel to "Walk with Jesus." A real highlight for me was sailing on the Sea of Galilee. I felt like I was living in the Gospels to be on the very same waters that Jesus sailed on and walked on! Of course, I recalled the story of the time that Jesus and his disciples were in their boat rowing when suddenly they got caught in a fierce storm.

Mark described what happened:

That day when evening came, [Jesus] said to his disciples, "Let us go over to the other side." Leaving the crowd behind, they took him along, just as he was, in the boat. There were also other boats with him. A furious squall came up, and the waves broke over the boat, so that it was nearly swamped. Jesus was in the stern, sleeping on a cushion. The disciples woke him and said to him, "Teacher, don't you care if we drown?"

He got up, rebuked the wind and said to the waves, "Quiet! Be still!" Then the wind died down and it was completely calm.

He said to his disciples, "Why are you so afraid? Do you still have no faith?"

They were terrified and asked each other, "Who is this? Even the wind and the waves obey him!" (Mark 4:35-41):

I Have to Fix This!
Dark storm clouds pelted torrents of freezing rain on Jesus and the disciples, gale winds whipped their boat in circles, and wave after wave splashed into them and was swamping their boat. The disciples were rowing and rowing as hard and fast as they could to get out of the furious squall and make it safely to land, but they couldn't make any progress – they were stuck in the middle of the sea about to capsize and drown!

The disciples were soaked in panic. They were drenched in doom. And Jesus was sleeping peacefully! Finally, they screamed at him in frustration: "Help Jesus! We're going to drown! Don't you care about us?"

How would *you* react if you were caught on a lake in a fierce storm? When you have a big problem how do you think about it? What belief system do you operate on when you're in trouble?
"It's up to me to fix this – I can't count on anyone else."
"If I don't solve this it'll be terrible."
"Why won't he/she help me!"
"I can't be happy until this problem is solved."

Many people I talk with who are in trouble think along those lines. They stress and worry until their problem is solved. They complain. They may panic, have an emotional melt down, or get angry at someone. They have no peace or joy until their situation improves. And it's up to them to fix things.

Maybe you relate? Maybe you get stressed out by difficulties. This "I have to fix my problem" mindset may become a script for your life, a storyline you live in, an habitual way of reacting to the distress in your life. Most people live with this belief system.

Life Events Stress Test

How is your stress level? What changes have you gone through in the last year that may be affecting your health and well-being? Health professionals have been using this highly researched "Life Events Stress Test" for over forty years. Countless people have taken it and found it very helpful.[23]

In the past 12 months, which of the following 43 major life events have taken place in your life? Place a check by each life event that you've experienced and then add up the points and total at the bottom. Then you can check how vulnerable you are to stress-related illness.

_____ 100 Death of Spouse
_____ 73 Divorce
_____ 65 Marital Separation or from relationship partner
_____ 63 Jail Term
_____ 63 Death of close family member
_____ 53 Personal injury or illness
_____ 50 Marriage
_____ 47 Fired from work
_____ 45 Marital reconciliation
_____ 45 Retirement
_____ 44 Change in family member's health

---

[23] Psychiatrists Thomas Holmes and Richard Rahe developed the "Holmes and Rahe Stress Scale" in 1967 after examining the medical records of over 5,000 medical patients as a way to determine whether stressful events might cause illnesses. They found a positive correlation as have subsequent research.

_____ 40 Pregnancy

_____ 39 Sex difficulties

_____ 39 Addition to family

_____ 39 Business readjustment

_____ 38 Change in financial status

_____ 37 Death of close friend

_____ 36 Change to a different line of work

_____ 35 Change in number of marital arguments

_____ 31 Mortgage or loan over $30,000

_____ 30 Foreclosure of mortgage or loan

_____ 29 Change in work responsibilities

_____ 29 Trouble with in-laws

_____ 28 Outstanding personal achievement

_____ 26 Spouse begins or stops work

_____ 26 Starting or finishing school

_____ 25 Change in living conditions

_____ 24 Revision of personal habits

_____ 23 Trouble with boss

_____ 20 Change in work hours, conditions

_____ 20 Change in residence

_____ 20 Change in schools

_____ 19 Change in recreational habits

_____ 19 Change in church activities

_____ 18 Change in social activities

_____ 17 Mortgage or loan under $20,000

_____ 16 Change in sleeping habits

_____ 15 Change in number of family gatherings

_____ 15 Change in eating habits

_____ 13 Vacation

_____ 12 Christmas season

_____ 11 Minor violations of the law

_____ Your Total Life Stress Score

Your Life Stress Score
0-149: Low susceptibility to stress-related illness

150-299: Medium susceptibility to stress-related illness

300 and over: High susceptibility to stress-related illness

Any change, even a positive one, is a stress that adds pressure on you. People who experience high levels of stress are vulnerable to stress related illness, especially if they internalize stress as anxiety or have difficulty coping with their stress.

Stress related health problems range from mild problems like frequent tension headaches, acid indigestion, loss of sleep to very serious illnesses like ulcers, hypertension, migraines, and cancer. Being overstressed can cause other problems too like anxiety disorders, depression, burn out, and conflicts in relationship.

The question of this chapter is, *How are you and I responding to the stress storms that we get caught in?* Most of us react to pressure and problems by trying harder to fix our problem in our own strength. But is this a right way to think? Is this helpful?

Celeste's Shattered Dream
Celeste told me that as long as she could remember her dream was to be married and to have a family. Seemingly every day she prayed for this when she was a girl, a teenager, in her 20's, and into her 30's. Now she was 42 and complaining to God as she sat in my office, "God, doesn't seem to care about me. I have served him and

been faithful to Christ, but he has not given me the desire of my heart."

For years Celeste had been active in her church singles group and she even used Christian dating services. She had read more books on Christian relationships than she could count. Her pastor and many others had prayed for her to be blessed with a good marriage. And prior to talking with me, she had worked with another Christian counselor for over a year getting help with her relationship issues and learning what she could do to grow as a Christian woman.

Looking back, Celeste could see that half a dozen serious boyfriends had come and gone in her life. When she opened her closet it was full of bridesmaid dresses, but there was not a wedding dress! She had lost hope that God would ever provide a match for her. She said she was afraid to become an "old maid" like her aunt who never did get married. And she was convinced that she was too old to have children.

It's not like Celeste was miserable. Every time she got worried or depressed about being single she picked herself up emotionally and counted her blessings: she had a busy social life with many good friends, appreciated her church family, went on mission trips, and loved her job as the Human Resource Director for a Christian nonprofit organization. But she used counting her blessings as a way to deny her grief and her repressed emotion developed into anxiety.

Celeste decided that she was on her own as it related to her longing to be married. Perhaps God really did care about her desires, but she concluded that he certainly wasn't actively helping her to find a godly husband. Her precious dream had slipped through her fingers and was lying on the ground in shattered pieces. This was the storm in her life and God was not calming it so she had to row harder and faster on her own to get to shore! It was up to her alone to develop a good dating relationship that would lead to marriage.

For a therapist I took a very unorthodox approach to helping Celeste. In addition to the obvious therapeutic work of helping her to grieve her losses, overcome self-condemnation, and develop better boundaries, I invited her to follow in the footsteps of Abraham who offered his beloved son Isaac on the altar of the Lord. Abraham let go of his dream into God's hands, trusting that his Lord had good purposes for him and could raise Isaac from the dead. He was able to do this because he *knew* the Lord as his Friend. God was enough for Abraham! Through trials like this he learned to find his peace and joy and meaning for life in the Lord (Genesis 22:1-19, Hebrews 11:17-19).

At first Celeste did not like the idea of going the way of Abraham. In frustration she said to me: "I've already given up on God bringing me a husband, but I can't give up trying myself! I can't give up my dream – it's the longing of my heart to be married. That makes it seem like God doesn't even love me!"

I asked Celeste to read the story of Abraham and to pray about it. After weeks of resisting, wrestling with God, crying, and praying she had a breakthrough in the middle of the night when she felt that God visited her in a special way. Afterward she told me: "Jesus is enough! I want him to be my First Love. I want to be his bride. Even if I never get married I can be happy if Jesus is my Friend and I walk closely with him."

I bet you know how the story ends! About four months after leaving her dream at the altar of the Lord, learning to accept her loss, and growing to delight more and more in Christ alone she met a wonderful Christian man through a friend. They got married. She became a stepmother and a year later they adopted a seven-year old girl. And they served the Lord together through their church.

Don't Worry about Waves – See Jesus' Smile!
Like Celeste, in my history I have often reacted to my problems by worrying, complaining, or getting frustrated. All I saw was the storm and so I worried about the waves that were threatening me. All I knew to do was to obsess on how I could fix things by rowing safely to shore. Perhaps I'd say a prayer, but generally I felt like I was on my own to deal with my problems. My reality was the storm. My identity was tied up in how I dealt with wind and waves. My solution was to work hard and smart to make things better for myself.

Then I looked closely at Jesus and saw him *smiling in the storm!*

How could Jesus sleep in the boat while the storm raged on? How could he be so *relaxed* (there's that word for Jesus again!) when he was rain-soaked, chilled to the bone, the disciples were yelling, and everyone was in great peril? He and his friends were about to drown! You might think he was calm because he was the Son of God and he knew he could calm the storm with a word. I don't think that's why.

Jesus was also a human being. The Bible tells us that Jesus was tempted in every way that we are, including to worry and to give into fear (Hebrews 4:15-16). And he was tempted to take matters into his own hands and act on his own, without the Father (Matthew 4:1-11).

So what's the answer? Why didn't the storm make Jesus afraid? How could be so calm in a crisis? Because *he was resting in his Abba's arms of love.*

You see, Jesus wasn't just in the visible storm – he was *in the invisible kingdom of the heavens.* He saw more than the waves – he saw his Father and many angels in action all around him. He heard more than thunder and the wind whipping the boat – he heard the words of his Father. He felt more than the cold wind and rain – he felt his Father's care.

So when Jesus awoke to face the storm he didn't command the wind and waves on his own. He simply said what he heard the Father saying, *as he always did* (John 14:10, 24). Jesus faced all kinds of trials, injustices, and hardships throughout his life and he didn't anxiously rush to fix these things on his own – instead he relied on the Father with him, rested in his easy yoke, and followed his lead.[24] This is why he was at peace in the life-threatening

---

[24] It wasn't only on the Cross and in the events leading up to it that Jesus endured trials with peace, joy, and love. He had many other storms to smile in: working as an ordinary carpenter serving customers for nearly two decades, losing his father at a young age, having his ministry rejected by his family and hometown friends, crowds of people trying to kill him, religious leaders constantly insulting him and plotting to kill him, disciples disagreeing with him, disciples turning

storm. Jesus' heart was full of divine peace and so it came out of him. It was the peace in Jesus that quieted the storm in the sea and also the one in the disciples' souls.

I Smiled in my Storm

Even now as I am writing *You Can Live in Jesus' Easy Yoke* a storm tested me. Looking back it was a far cry from a hurricane – it was just a little thundercloud that pelted me, but in the moment I felt attacked. A Christian leader condemned me as a heretic for teaching that mere people could actually become more like the Son of God and using "contemplative spirituality." On his website he posted a picture of my wife and I and he made disparaging remarks about us. Clearly, he would be quite upset if when he got to heaven he found out that I was his roommate! Especially if I invited him to meditate on a Psalm with me!

For this man to disagree with our doctrine was okay – on some points he might be right and I might be wrong – but the *contempt* for my lovely wife and me that he spewed out to the world was hurtful! In my nature I am eager to do good and to please other people and I am sensitive to criticism. So in years past my normal reaction to being harshly judged, especially in public by an intelligent Christian leader, was to scurry to fix my reputation so I didn't have to be embarrassed (which is the deceitful and stress-inducing "I have to fix this myself!" mentality). Or I might get angry. But in this case I did neither.

---

away from following him, kings and ordinary folk alike mocking him, and constant ministry pressures from one needy person after another.

By God's grace I thanked God that I was being persecuted for Christ – *and* that this Christian leader had devoted himself to teaching others Biblical doctrine as best he could. I prayed for God's blessing on this man and his ministry, that God would draw him closer to Christ, encourage and help him in his study of Christian doctrine, and use him to bring more and more people into God's truth for life.

I believe that Christ came out of my heart quite naturally in this trial (I wish this was always the case!) because for some years now Christ has been teaching me to do all that I do in God's kingdom. This includes regularly praying Psalms of Lament and other Scriptures in which I practice relaxing in Abba's arms in anticipation of coming storms and then when the storms hit I'm already rejoicing in God's kingdom and less prone to react with stress or agitation.

It is only Jesus' Easy Yoke Gospel that sets us free to smile in our storms, but few people today understand, much less live in terms of, the Gospel that Jesus preached.

The Gospels we Commonly Hear Today
For many years Dallas Willard has asked people, "Why is it that so many Christians today don't look much like Christ?" He says it is because they believe a different gospel than the one Jesus preached – they don't know and trust *his* gospel.[25] I know that this was true of me for most of my Christian life. Even many of our best Bible teachers

---

[25] My understanding of the different false gospels and Jesus' Gospel is from Dallas Willard. See his watershed book, *Divine Conspiracy.*

today don't present Jesus' Gospel. If this is true then it's no wonder why much Bible teaching today (as wise and helpful as it can be) doesn't seem to make disciples to Jesus.

There are different gospels in the Church today…

The Conservative Gospel on the Right:
"Believe the right facts about Jesus and you'll be forgiven of your sin and let into heaven when you die."

Jesus died to pay for our sins and rose from the dead if we will only believe this then we will be forgiven of our sins and go to heaven when we die. Getting our doctrinal facts right (e.g., by studying the Bible) removes our guilt and gets us into heaven when we die.

The Social Gospel on the Left:
"Love other people, especially the poor and needy, and God will accept you and let you into heaven when you die."

Jesus came and gave his life to love the oppressed, liberating them to be all that they can be. Ministries of compassion and healing, support groups, counseling, and other ways of helping hurting people as Jesus did is *the* purpose of life and how we get into heaven.

Consumer Christianity:
"Ask God and he'll bless you like you want. He'll help make your project of a successful life turn out. Go to church to get your needs met and feel better. Take care of your church and it will take care of you."

We use God's grace for the forgiveness we need and the blessings we want. The church is our spiritual shopping mall in which we "buy" whatever services we need to take care of ourselves or to get God to take care of us. We expect the services of the church to entertain us and to meet our "felt needs" and in turn the church expects us to give money and use our gifts to help serve.

Jesus' Gospel of the Kingdom of God

Each of these three Gospels *is* partially true! But they miss the mark. What's missing? The heart of Jesus's Gospel of the Kingdom of God is missing: submit yourself to Jesus Christ the Lord, in all that you do, abandoning all outcomes to him, trusting his good purposes for you. In the other gospels I am still in charge of my daily life activities; I am fixing what's wrong with *my* doctrine, *my* good works, or *my* efforts to get my needs met.

What is the kingdom of God? Dallas Willard answers that a "kingdom" simply is the effective range of someone's will. You and I have a kingdom or queendom – things, activities, and even people that we're in charge of. For instance, if someone starts rummaging through your purse or your wallet you feel violated, "Het, that's mine! What are you doing?" That's part of your kingdom that you've been given responsibility for.

God's kingdom is simply God in action; it's where what God wants done is done, which is why Jesus taught us to pray to the Father, "Thy kingdom come, Thy will be done on earth as it is in heaven" (Matthew 6:10).

But we tend to think of God's kingdom as being *far off and way later.* When we speak of the kingdom of God it's usually in reference to heaven. We've been taught that the people of the first century rejected Jesus' kingdom and so now we all have to wait until we go to heaven or when Jesus returns to earth to enter his kingdom. So in this life we're left to "hang on" in our struggle with sin and keep going to God for his forgiveness while we wait for future peace and glory. It's like we've had car trouble and we had to pull off to the side of the highway while we wait for the heavenly AAA to come get us and take us home to heaven.

Jesus' Gospel, his Good News, is that each one of us has the opportunity to become his apprentice in his kingdom. Jesus' offer is clear: "Repent for the kingdom of the heavens[26] is at hand" (Matthew 4:17). In other words, Jesus is saying to you and I:

> Think again about how you're living your life. Review your strategy for life in the light of this wonderful new opportunity that God's kingdom is open to you: you are loved by the King of kings! Hold onto life on your terms and you're living an

---

[26] According to Dallas Willard in *Divine Conspiracy* Matthew uses the term "kingdom of heavens" rather than the "kingdom of God" to emphasize *the direct and immediately availability of the Lord's rule* – he is always right beside us and his Spirit lives within us who trust in him! And there are angles among us too! Note that we are speaking of heavens in the plural, which is the better translation in Matthew and in most uses throughout the Bible (See Young's Literal Translation of the Bible at BibleGateway.com.) The Hebrew concept is that there are seven levels to heaven and the lowest level of the heavens is immediately present in the air we breathe. Similarly, in Ephesians Paul refers to the wonderful blessings of our position "in Christ" – or in the kingdom of God – as being in the "heavenly realms" (plural) because there are levels to the heavens (1:3, 1:20, 2:6).

empty, loveless, dead life. But lose your life for me and you'll discover real, abundant life. Run your life as you see fit and you'll get nowhere. But submit to me – ask me to govern your thoughts, desires, and all that you say and do – and you'll learn how to live your ordinary life today in the reality of the heavenly realms with me now and forever. (My paraphrase of Jesus' gospel.)

Jesus' point is that *if you want to go to heaven when you die then don't wait – go now!* If heaven starts to get into you now then getting into heaven when you die will take care of itself. The Savior, the Holy One, who sacrificed himself for us, offers us God's kind of life – real and abundant life – that begins just as soon as we offer our lives to him, submitting to his kingdom rule. What Good News this is that we don't have to fix our own problems or just hang on in our difficult life till we die and go to heaven, but we can actually grow in the blessings of God's grace and righteousness now as we submit to Jesus Christ and rely on him. (It is important to say that Jesus' kingdom being available to us now does not deny that in eternity there will be for us a glorious new manifestation of God's kingdom on earth and in heaven!)

Our opportunity is to let our kingdom be taken over by God's kingdom, to submit our will to the will of our Father, to do all that we do with the Lord and according to his leadership. In this way we not only enjoy the benefits of God's kingdom but we are also prepared and empowered to minister his kingdom – his caring rule – to other people.

The Gospel of the Kingdom is *the* New Testament Gospel
The Gospel Jesus preached remained, "Think again about how you're living your life in light of your opportunity to turn and enter God's kingdom" (my paraphrase). Again and again – over 100 times in the Gospels! – Jesus invited people to participate in God's kingdom. He communicates this through parables, healings, and teaching. Of course, he varies his wording, but his theme does not change. When he was resurrected and appeared to his disciples over 40 days he continued to talk to them about life in the kingdom of God (Acts 1:3). He did not change his message to say, "Since all the people have rejected me as their king everyone will have to wait to enter my kingdom until my second coming or until they die and go to heaven."

Jesus trained his disciples to preach and manifest his Gospel of the Kingdom in the same way that he did: "As you go, proclaim the good news, 'The kingdom of heaven has come near.' Cure the sick, raise the dead, cleanse the lepers, cast out demons" (Matthew 10:5-8).

Some theologians say that the Apostle Paul did not preach a Gospel of the Kingdom. But Acts records him talking to people "persuasively about the kingdom of God" (Acts 19:8) and "welcoming all who came to him, proclaiming the kingdom of God and teaching about the Lord Jesus Christ with all boldness and without hindrance" (Acts 28:30-31). Fourteen times in his epistles Paul teaches explicitly on the kingdom of God. For instance he says: "For [God] has rescued us from the dominion of darkness and brought us into the kingdom of the Son he loves, in whom we have redemption, the forgiveness of sins" (Colossians 1:13-14).

The Gospel of the Kingdom is Countercultural

Jesus spoke bold words, offensive to many people, when he said: "I am the way and the truth and the life. No one comes to the Father except through me" (John 14:6). But I'm afraid that you and I who believe these words and call ourselves "Christ-followers" may, nonetheless, be prone to follow *the way* of our culture in some aspects, more than *the way* of Christ, particularly when we face the challenges and stresses of our lives.

More than we realize, a false gospel may be influencing our mindset and attitudes. Consider how eager we are to turn to self-help gurus, wise counselors, motivating coaches, inspiring speakers, and various other professionals and experts to help us *get what we want* out of our lives, relationships, jobs, or ministries. Perhaps we are more likely to learn Biblical principles as proven techniques to succeed, rather than as ways to *grow in our discipleship to Jesus and advance his kingdom.*

When we have a problem in our family, organization, or church who is our first and primary consultant? Who do we rely on for help and to give us advice? Probably an expert or a professional. We may not even have the thought that *Jesus is the smartest Person alive and he is available to consult with!*[27] Our Lord and Savior is also our Wonderful Counselor and in him are hid all treasures of wisdom and knowledge (Isaiah 9:6, Colossians 2:3). As we

---

[27] Dallas Willard writes, "If you ask evangelicals to pick the smartest man in the world, very few of them will list Jesus Christ... How can you be a disciple of someone you don't think of as really bright?" *The Great Omission: Reclaiming Jesus' Essential Teachings on Disicpleship* (Harper: 2006), p. 168.

do whatever we're doing we can step into his kingdom of God classroom and as his students we can learn from him how he would do what we're doing if he were us.

Am I being too harsh? Look closely at the book titles on our Christian Best Seller Lists or notice the commercials on Christian radio and television and you will see what I am talking about. In our generation we "Christians" are more likely to put our efforts and prayers into *trying to get God to help us make our project of a successful life turn out the way we want it to* than we are to absorb ourselves with living as disciples of Jesus.

Please don't misunderstand me. I do not mean to say that is bad to seek help from professionals and experts! (Remember that I am a Psychologist!) My point is this: when you go to a consultant look to him or her as Christ's Ambassador to you – pray and listen for God's guidance through this person. And even before you pick up a self-help book or call on an expert (and then while you do those things) consult with the Lord Jesus Christ, listen to him and follow his lead.

In other words, step into the easy yoke of Jesus! *It's the best life possible* and it opens to you when you *submit* to the King who is kind rather than trying to make things happen for yourself (or "for God"!).

What Celeste Learned
Celeste was following the way of the culture when she was trying to make her marriage dream come true. But when she let go and laid her dream down at the Altar of the Lord she was submitting to the Lord and trusting his rule in her life in a new way. She took her frustration over dating, her

grief that she was still single, and her fear of being an "old maid" into God's kingdom and discovered that *the Lord was her portion* – even if she was still single and without a child.

Have *you* experienced the reality that living in submission to the kind governance of Jesus Christ *is* the blessed life – even if other things in your life are not going well? Have you learned that even in the midst of storms not yet calmed you can smile with Jesus and be at rest in the Father's arms of love? Do you know how to walk in the easy yoke of Jesus through your trials? Is God really enough for you?

"The Lord is my portion!" the Psalmist extolled repeatedly in the midst of his sufferings. No matter what happens God is enough! That's the implication of Jesus' Gospel of the kingdom that eradicates the damaging and pressure-filled mindset of "I have to fix my problems myself."

In summary, the way into this Gospel life of peace and joy that Celeste learned is to:
- Believe Jesus' gospel that we can smile in our storm
- Practice the discipline of *always* being thankful to God for God and his kingdom
- Accept our daily life problems as tests of character that show us where we're at and what we need to work on in with Christ in order to become more like him[28]

---

[28] These three points make up the Triangle of Soul Transformation that I presented in the Introduction.

Spiritual Exercise: Give Thanks in Trials

Jesus told us to expect troubles and to "take heart" from him and how he dealt with them (Matthew 9:22, 22; Mark 6:50; John 16:33). And in their many persecutions and sufferings the Apostles followed this example of our Lord. Paul taught, "Give thanks in all circumstances for this is God's will for you in Christ Jesus" (1 Thessalonians 5:18). James, the brother of our Lord, agreed, "Consider it pure joy... whenever you face trials of many kinds" (James 1:2). Peter also urged us to praise God in difficult and painful situations (1 Peter 1:3-9).

Being thankful when we have problems? Having "pure joy" in pain and injustice? Praising God when things go wrong?

William Law[29] (1686-1761), an evangelical devotional writer of three centuries ago from the Anglican tradition, understood giving thanks to God in trials. The Englishman gave up a promising career as a priest in the university or the church when he refused to swear allegiance to the new monarch. He settled for working as a tutor and a

---

[29] William Law also established and lived the last 21 years of his life in a special fellowship (it was a small disciplined society that was like an informal monastery) of sincere Protestant Christians united in prayer and charity. He encouraged all Christians who to grow in their devotion to the Lord and their readiness to obey him by participating in Christian community and practicing spiritual disciplines.

Law's famous work, *A Serious Call to a Devout and Holy Life*, is on the short list of the great classics of Christian devotion. John Wesley called it one of three books which accounted for his first "explicit resolve to be all devoted to God."

writer. He accepted his unfortunate lot with a positive attitude and urged others to follow his example:

> There is no state of mind so holy, so excellent, and so truly perfect as that of thankfulness to God. Consequently, nothing is of more importance in religion than that which exercises and improves this habit of mind. The greatest saint in the world is he who is always thankful to God, who wills everything God wills, who receives everything as an instance of God's goodness, and who has a heart always ready to praise God...

If anyone would tell you the shortest, surest way to all happiness and all perfection, he must tell you to make a rule to yourself to thank and praise God for everything that happens to you... This thankful spirit... heals and turns all that it touches into happiness.

> For this reason I exhort you to this method in your devotion that every day may be made a day of thanksgiving, and that the spirit of murmur and discontent may be unable to enter into the heart that is so often employed in singing the praises of God.[30]

But it's not natural to be happy when you're having troubles! Like me, you've tried coping with your stress in your own strength and probably you were not joyful in doing so! Most of us know from personal experience what

---

[30] William Law, *A Serious Call to a Devout and Holy Life,* written in 1728, p. 101.

it's like to be anxiously consumed with trying to fix our problems (or other people's problems). And we know what it's like to respond to our difficulties, not with thanks to God, but with complaining, worrying, or getting discouraged.

Or we may compare our troubles to those of other people, cheering ourselves up if we have it better than them or feeling sorry for ourselves if we have it worse. God's wisdom for us is not to compare ourselves to others (either up or down), but to test our own actions to see if they're good and to be responsible for our own life before God (Galatians 6:4-5). The thing to compare our personal suffering with is *the good that God is working in us* and in that analysis the Bible teaches us that our troubles our "light and momentary" and the image of Christ that God is forming in us is "an eternal glory that outweighs them all" – this is what we "fix our eyes on" and it is how we are "renewed day by day" (2 Corinthians 4:16-18). Indeed, hope dawns for us when we pray along these lines:

> Lord Jesus, you are wonderful to me and you are doing something good that I'm not yet seeing. So I'm watching to see what you're doing in this situation and what you want to teach me. I'm ready to join with you in the work of your kingdom and to follow you however you lead me in this trial.

Peter elaborated on why we can thank God in the middle of our trials, saying that by God's mercy through Christ we have been given "new birth into a living hope" – the hope of enjoying the glory of heaven with the Lord forever *and* the "inexpressible and glorious joy" that right now we are receiving the salvation of souls (1 Peter 1:3-9).

In other words, what brings us joy in our trials is that *we are alive in God's kingdom now and forever!* Christ the Lord and King is with us, loving us and shaping us in his image, refining our faith like gold tried in the fire (1 Peter 1:7). We are with our Lord and he is developing us to grow in our intimacy with him and our capacity to partner with him in his work. We may suffer great losses, injustices, or pain and from the world's perspective things may not go well for us. But if we realize that we are living and growing in the kingdom of the heavens – and therefore do not need to be overwhelmed by or defined by our problem situation – then we have reason to be *wonderfully happy!*

The way to be happy in God during our trials is to *practice it,* cultivating a joyful-faith-in-Christ-mindset to bring into our perspective on our problems. Jesus' beatitudes help us to do this.

Meditate on Jesus' Beatitudes

We have misunderstood Jesus' beatitudes.[31] Before I say anymore I want to ask you to open your mind and heart to the *possibility* that the teaching you have been given about the beatitudes is off. At first you may disagree with what I'm going to say. I did too when it was first presented to me. But after searching the Scriptures, thinking about it, and praying I concluded that this new understanding was right – it fit Jesus' Gospel and the context of the Sermon on the Mount and it was more helpful to my life!

---

[31] I learned this understanding of Jesus' beatitudes from Dallas Willard in *Divine Conspiracy.*

Like everyone else I knew I used to read the beatitudes as *prescriptions* for obtaining God's blessings. We think Jesus is giving us *conditions* that we must meet in order to have a God-blessed life. So we try to use them to *engineer* our way to be happier, to get what we want from God. But God's blessings don't work that way! We don't make them happen! And it is a burden to try to force ourselves into poverty (physical or spiritual), mourning, persecution, and all the other examples of difficulty that Jesus refers to in the beatitudes.

Thankfully, Jesus is not telling us to try to be poor in spirit! He is not telling us to cry more, or get ourselves mistreated. He is saying that the Good News of his Gospel is available to you even if you are poor in spirit, grieving, persecuted, or disadvantaged in some other way. He is pronouncing the availability of God's kingdom on people who for one reason or another do not feel blessed or even eligible ever to be blessed. Jesus is saying to you and me and anyone who will listen that in the midst of whatever pain or problem we might have the wonders and joys of God's kingdom are greater than those difficulties and they are available to us immediately!

With Jesus we can smile in our storm!

Jesus' teaching is upside down from what we expect and from the way things work in our world. This is especially clear in Luke's version of the beatitudes: "Blessed are you who are poor... hungry... weeping... hated." What is the blessing in being poor? Not having enough food to eat? Suffering a terrible loss? Being hated by people? *Nothing.* Obviously, these conditions are not desirable. And it is natural and proper to do what we can to alleviate our suffering. But the critical lesson for us to learn is that *even in bad situations that are not resolved, or may never resolve until we get to heaven, we can learn to "leap for joy" because we are a part of God's kingdom and rewarded by God our Father* (Luke 6:20-23).

Jesus' inversions in the beatitudes are actually the right side up view; it only seems to us to be upside down if we have been indoctrinated by our culture. If we immerse ourselves in the mind of Christ and in our appreciation of being immediately a part of God's glorious kingdom then we will learn to readily rejoice in life and to continue rejoicing when we come into trials.

My paraphrases of Jesus' beatitudes in Matthew's gospel have helped me to accept my trials and joyfully submit to God's kingdom work in me and through me. Many other people have found similar encouragement. I invite you to join us in praying through Jesus' beatitudes by reading each one *meditatively* and relating it to your own life...

A crowd of people came to Jesus. He climbed a hillside with his disciples and taught all the people:

Blessed are those who are uneducated in the spiritual life, for the kingdom of the heavens is available to them.

Blessed are those who are grieving a terrible loss, for the Lord's comfort is here for them also.

Blessed are the shy and unassertive, for they too are offered heaven's best blessing on earth.

Blessed are those who are wrongly treated and long for justice, for the Lord is eager to fill them with his goodness.

Blessed are the sensitive-hearted who are burdened by others' pain, for the Lord's unfailing mercy is available to them.

Blessed are the nice people who are last in line, for the Lord sees their hearts and wants to befriend them too.

Blessed are those who get in the middle of conflicts to try to bring peace, for the Lord calls them his sons and daughters.

Blessed are those who are persecuted for being godly and doing right, for the kingdom of the heavens is available to them (Matthew 5:1-10, paraphrase).

Write out your own "Blesseds"
To participate in the full benefit of the Gospel blessings that Jesus pronounces on us we need to apply the *spirit* of them to whatever particular difficult circumstances we're dealing with in our lives today. Try writing out a few of your own *personal beatitudes* from God that relate to the trials you're experiencing. As the storm around you rages and the waves are thrashing your boat appreciate that Jesus Christ, the Lord and King, is with you and he is at peace. With Christ in charge you too can smile in your storm!

Make a list of your problems that you wish you didn't have.
These may be issues you've been praying for God's help with. Don't minimize an issue you're struggling with just because other people have worse problems.

Maybe the problem you're having trouble accepting has to do with a money shortage, stress at work, health crisis, emotional struggle, criticism from others, family problem, injustice you're experiencing, unfulfilled dream...

Go to prayer.
One at a time lay your burden before Jesus by sharing honestly with him about your struggle. Admit to any doubts or unmet expectations...

Say the Blesseds.
For each difficulty, hear Jesus say to you, *"Blessed are you __(your name)__ in/with __(your problem)__ for yours is the kingdom of heaven."*

In other words, though it's certainly *not* a blessing to have a health problem or to be short of money *it is a wonderful blessing to realize that in the midst of the trial that Jesus is your King and you can live with him under his kind rule!*

For instance, I prayed these personal beatitudes:
"Blessed are you Bill with financial uncertainties for the abundance of God's Kingdom is available to you now and forever."
"Blessed are you Bill when you are criticized for you are embraced in the Father's love."
"Blessed are you Bill with Irritable Bowel Syndrome and the pain it causes you for the peace of Christ is for you."

Breath Prayer
Our Breath Prayer from Scripture this week is the words of Jesus in the storm: "Peace. Be still."

In the spirit of Jesus' kingdom beatitudes we want to meditate on his words of peace to help us shift our focus from struggling to get out of our personal storm to *learning to rest in our Abba Father's arms with Jesus in the midst of our storm.* Breathing in and out the blessed peace of Christ can help us to take it deeper into our hearts (our will and orientation for life) so that it becomes more a part of us and overflows from us to the people we intersect with each day.

Take a few minutes or more while lying in bed, in a quiet chair, while you're driving or waiting for someone, or as you take a walk to meditate on Jesus' words: "Peace. Be Still" (Mark 4:39). To help you focus you may want to imagine the Gospel story of Jesus sleeping in the boat, resting in Abba's arms, as the storm raged on and on. See the calm sea in Jesus' soul in the midst of all the turmoil and danger going on all around him. Pray "Peace. Be still." Pray to be more like Jesus

You might try breathing Jesus' words in and out: "Peace. Be still." Breathe in slow and deep: "Peace..." Hold your breath... Exhale: "Be still..."

Fill your *spiritual* lungs with the Word and the Spirit... Hold them around your heart... Release and relax... Repeat this prayer till you sense the reality of God's peace inside your soul.

Then talk to the Lord Jesus about one of your stormy trials. Imagine yourself in this situation. Then meditate on Jesus' words: "Peace... Be still..."

When you're time of focused, quiet prayer is over take your Breath Prayer with you as you do whatever you're doing. As often as you can remember practice God's presence by praying with Jesus: "Peace... Be still..." And ask God to help you bring his peace to help you calm the souls of the people you encounter today. You can do this with encouraging words or by praying silently for them, "Peace... Be still..."

Salty Questions

Jesus said, "You're here to be salt-seasoning that brings out the God-flavors of this earth. If you lose your saltiness, how will people taste godliness?" (Matthew 5:13, MSG). It's time for some "salt seasoned" conversation to bring out the God-flavor in you and your friends who are on the *Easy Yoke* journey with you. Being salty will also help you and your friends to preserve what God is teaching you, while at the same time making you thirsty for more of God in your lives.

What is one thing you learned about Jesus' kingdom gospel?

What is a problem that you're being challenged by this week? What personal beatitude does the Lord have for you in your trial?

What effect did receiving Jesus' beatitude and/or meditating on his words "Peace... Be still" have on your ability to rejoice in the midst of a problem this week?

You Can Live in Jesus' Easy Yoke: Lesson #3
Jump into Abba's Arms

Some years ago I had a delightful experience that I'll never forget. I was about to drive home from an appointment and I called home first. My youngest daughter, Briana, who was seven years old at the time, answered and I told her that I would be home in five minutes and that I had a hug to give her.

When I walked in the door she was waiting for me on the couch and she jumped up and ran toward me, shouting out, "433 seconds! 433 seconds!"

"What do you mean?" I asked with bewilderment.

"It took you 433 seconds to get home Daddy!" And she leaped up into my arms...

Just telling the story melts my heart all over again, even many years later... How blessed I am to have a daughter who loves me like that!

All three of my kids when they were little would do things like that. Now they're teenagers, but that's another story! As little children when they heard me open the door they'd yell from our family room in the back of the house, "Daddy's home!" And then they'd say, "Daddy, wait there at the door." And then one-by-one they'd sprint the full length of the house and jump into my arms for a hug!

Sometimes this ritual was followed by what we came to call "Rough and Tough," which was a game of chasing the kids around the house to catch them in order to wrestle, tickle, and throw them onto a couch.

These are very special memories in part because my Dad did the same thing with me. The "Daddy's home!" moment was often the highlight of my day as a little boy too.

Now I want to ask you (and myself!) a question...

Would you count the seconds before you could jump into the arms of your Heavenly Father? Is being Jesus' disciple the delight of your heart? Can you imagine becoming a person like that?

Many people I talk to don't like God that much. They are not sure about jumping into the arms of God their Father.

Jessica Didn't Trust God

"I can't *really* trust God," Jessica admitted to me. She couldn't imagine jumping with delight into the arms of God. She was a Christian and in her doctrine she believed in Christ and in the goodness of God, but in her heart she didn't feel safe depending on God.

"Where was God when my father sexually abused me?" she cried. "How could God allow seven years of letting my body be used for my father's perversion? I was just a little girl. I didn't even know what sex was. He damaged me beyond repair.

"It's so confusing to me. The same dad who made me laugh and bought me nice things abused me! And, worst of all, he made me feel physical pleasure about something so gross! Then to add to the shame of it all, later I acted this out by getting into sexual relationships, not only with boyfriends, but even with a married man. I'm so mad about this! My life has been ruined!"

Many nights Jessica cried out to God that the dark shadow wouldn't come into her room again, but it kept coming back. And when it did she froze in mute fear. She endured the pain by dissociating, pretending she wasn't there, shutting down her emotion.

Her father threatened her that if she ever told anyone about their "special secret" that she'd be sent away from the family. A few times she took the risk of trying to tell her mother, but she didn't believe her. This "special secret" was really a "dirty secret". Who could she tell? Her pet cat – *really*. Jessica's cat listened to her cry and purred in her lap. No one else knew.

Jessica's image of God was that he had a mean side like her father. And she also saw God as passive like her mom because he allowed her to be violated.

I've talked with many dozens of people whose image of God has been painfully damaged not only by childhood abuse of one kind or another, but also by emotional neglect or hypocrisy in a parent, pastor, or other Christian teacher. When you're vulnerable and your trust is wounded repeatedly it's hard to recover, it doesn't feel safe to trust again.

"I Can't *Really* Trust Anyone"
If you were Jessica could you trust God? Imagine yourself in her position – because perhaps more than you want to

admit you are. To one degree or another, we've all trusted and been wounded or disappointed in life. It may have been through your parents divorcing, a care-giver dying, a family conflict, a loved one's addiction, a spouse cheating on you, or a friend disappearing in a time of need. Most of us try to minimize our pain and problems by comparing ourselves to people like Jessica who seem to have had a harder life. But this is *not* helpful. We need to be honest before God and one another about any hurts or injustices that have shaped our heart's ability to trust and our view of God.

We might say that we "know" God is loving, but in our hearts, in our life experience, do we *truly know* God as good and kind? We say that we trust God, but deep down inside do we trust him enough to submit ourselves *completely* to him? Maybe we feel that in some ways we need to hold back on being vulnerable with others and rely on ourselves.

When I listen to people and get down below the surface and into their hearts I find that often they believe along the lines of these narratives:
"Be strong. Don't cry."
"Children are to be seen, not heard"
"Grin and bear it till the pain goes away."
"Don't be needy – you'll burden people."
"You have to watch your back!"
"Pull yourself up by the bootstraps!"

Believing that you can't trust anyone shrinks your heart. To whatever extent you hold back from being vulnerable with the safe people who are accessible to you then you are missing out on the love you need and you'll be diminished in your capacity to love others fully.

You might think that you can trust God without trusting people, but it doesn't work that way. Jesus makes this point in his Greatest Commandment that links loving the God who loves us and loving our neighbor as ourselves (Mark 12:29-30). The Apostle John in his first letter goes to great lengths to teach about the inseparable connection between how we relate with God and how we relate to other people (1 John 3:17-18, 4:11-12).

We learn to trust the God we can't see by trusting people that we can see. This begins at birth as David said to the Lord, "I learned to trust in you at my mother's breast" (Psalm 22:9). When we've been emotionally wounded by people we experience repair by finding someone that we can trust and sharing our heart and learning to do this as unto Christ. This is why in the Bible Christians are called "the body of Christ" (1 Corinthians 12:27) or "Christ's Ambassadors" (2 Corinthians 5:20).

When you have heart wounds that haven't been healed or developmental needs that haven't been met it profoundly affects how you view God – how much you really trust him – and how you live and relate to others.

What is Your Image of God?

I developed the God Image Questionnaire (GIQ) to help people better understand how they see and experience God on a personal level.[32] To assess your inner, emotional

---

[32] The *God Image Questionnaire* is based on my Ph.D. dissertation that I did in 1989. I revised some of the wording of the GIQ in 2000.

concept of God each question asks about your "feelings" in your relationship with God. Do not answer the questions according to your opinions or theological beliefs about God. In other words, don't just give the "right" answers! Respond according to your *personal experience of God* or how you actually tend to relate to God.

Read each question and then circle "T" for true and "F" for false.

- At times I feel that God doesn't give His full attention to the details of my life.   T   F
- When I need God it sometimes feels like He does not help me very much.   T   F
- I feel like God sometimes withholds good things from me.   T   F
- I feel disregarded by God at times.   T   F
- I feel that God is distant from me.   T   F
- At times I feel pressured to do something for God that I don't want to do.   T   F
- I feel I have to do something to obtain God's favor.   T   F
- To please God I feel I must measure up to His expectations.   T   F
- When I confess my sin I don't always feel forgiven by God.   T   F
- At times it feels unfair the way God treats me.   T   F
- If I'm in a threatening situation I tend to feel unprotected by God.   T   F
- I feel that my abilities are unimportant to God.   T   F

- I feel unsure about whether or not God has a purpose for my future.   T   F
- When I really need God I tend to feel left on my own.   T   F
- I feel that I may be a bother to God if I talk to Him about a decision I need to make. T   F
- I feel that I don't get enough help with my problems from God.   T   F
- At times I feel deprived of good things by God.   T   F
- I feel insignificant to God.   T   F
- I feel removed from God.   T   F
- Sometimes I feel controlled by God. T   F
- If I want God to do something for me then it feels like it helps my cause to do something for Him.   T   F
- I feel disapproved of by God.   T   F
- After I tell God I am sorry I still feel He may be upset with me.   T   F
- I feel harshly judged by God sometimes.   T   F
- If someone tries to take advantage of me I tend to feel undefended by God.   T   F
- I feel that my abilities are doubted by God.   T   F
- I fee unsure of whether or not God has special plans for my future.   T   F
- In difficult times it feels like God isn't at my side.   T   F

Scoring: To score and understand your GIQ use the table below. It has 14 rows, one for each of the 14 aspects of God's perfect love from 1 Corinthians 13:4-7. (The first word or term for each aspect of love is from the NIV translation and the other words are my definitions.) There are two questions ("Quest") for each aspect.

"False" answers to any question on the GIQ indicate a generally and usually positive experience of God's love (or image of God) in that particular aspect.

Follow these four steps:
Circle each of the 28 questions that you answered with "false."

Count one point for each "false" answer.

Add up the total for each row (aspect of God's perfect love). Scores should range from 0 to 2. Scores of 2 indicate your God Image strengths, areas where you have a positive experience of that aspect of God's love. Scores of 0 indicate your God Image weaknesses, areas where you're struggling to feel God's love and need help.

Add up your total GIQ score for all 14 rows combined. Scores should range from 0 to 28. Higher scores mean a closer and more loving relationship with God, an image of God that is more positive and true to the God of the Bible.

Question	Aspect of God's Love	Score
1, 15	Patient: attentive, interested	
2, 16	Kind: helpful	
3, 17	Not envious: generous, gives good gifts	
4, 18	Not boastful: esteems and shows regard	
5, 19	Not proud: close, available	
6, 20	Not rude: gives freedom, gentle	
7, 21	Not self-seeking: unconditional favor and Care	
8, 22	Not easily angered: considerate of Weaknesses	
9, 23	No record of wrongs: forgiving, merciful	
10, 24	Rejoices in truth, not evil: fair, does what's Right	
11, 25	Protects: keeps safe, defends	
12, 26	Trusts: respects, believes in abilities	
13, 27	Hopeful: has good plan and purpose	
14, 28	Perseveres: reliable, faithful	
	GIQ TOTAL:	

O to See God as He is!
We all tend to project onto God from our life experience. Our heart's view of God is readily shaped by the way that our parents and other caregivers related to us early in life. As little people we internalize the messages that are spoken or implicit and then these color the lenses we use to view others, particularly God. For instance, a man who is emotionally detached says, "God is distant from me." Or a woman who struggles with anger, including at herself, experiences God as harsh and punitive.

A.W. Tozer[33] (1897-1963), one of the greatest pastors and writers of the 20th Century, wrote:

> What comes into our minds when we think about God is the most important thing about us...

That our idea of God corresponds as nearly as possible to the true being of God is of immense importance to us. Compared with our actual thoughts about Him, our creedal statements are of little consequence. Our real idea of God may lie buried under the rubbish of conventional religious notions and may require an intelligent and vigorous search before it is finally unearthed and exposed for what it is. Only after an ordeal of painful self-probing

---

[33] A.W. Tozer was a Christian Missionary & Alliance Pastor and author of 40 Christian books, including his classic of Christian devotion, *The Pursuit of God*. Tozer never attended Bible College or seminary, but was Spirit-taught and Spirit-filled to become a man who loved and served Christ with unrelenting passion. He is considered an "Evangelical Mystic" because the fire of whole-hearted devotion to Christ burns hot in his prayers and message.

are we likely to discover what we actually believe about God.

A right conception of God is basic not only to systematic theology but to practical Christian living as well...

The man [or woman] who comes to a right belief about God is relieved of ten thousand temporal problems.[34]

Because we see God "through a glass darkly" and only "know in part" the Apostle Paul in 1 Corinthians 13 tried to bring home for us the teaching that God is love, perfect love. He emphasized over and over how we need to "love one another" in the Body of Christ – we are to be Christ to one another, to incarnate God's grace for one another. This is a primary way that Christ heals our hurts and clears up our image of God so that we can grow to trust God from our hearts and appreciate his love.

Why Does God Allow Unjust Suffering?
Do you trust that God has always been good to you? Are you confident that his love for you is unfailing? Here's a litmus test: Look back over your personal history and consider times you were mistreated or experienced hardship... Can you see God caring for you despite your circumstances to the contrary? Can you say honestly and gratefully, "The Lord has been good to me!"? Or try this test: How do you react when you see or hear about a child starving in Africa or a drunk driver killing a teenager? Are you able to trust that God genuinely and immediately cares for the one in peril?

---

[34] A. W. Tozer, Knowledge of the Holy, 1961, p. 1-2.

This issue causes problems for many people. Why does a good and powerful God allow innocent people to suffer? This is an age-old question! And many forests have been cut down to print books that discuss this issue. The Bible itself, in the Psalms and elsewhere, wrestles with the question of innocent people suffering many, many times. In all instances God doesn't answer our why question directly, not even when Jesus borrows the words of David from Psalm 22:1 and cries out, while being tortured to death on the cross: "My God, my God why have you forsaken me?"

Jesus on the cross *is* God's response to the pain and injustice that we suffer from. And on the cross and throughout his life Jesus shows us – as did the prophets before him and the apostles after him – that we need to learn to draw our joy, meaning, and identity not from the visible world, but from the invisible one, from the larger, glorious and eternal reality of God's kingdom in our midst. And from that perspective of knowing the immediate spiritual reality of God's loving presence and purposes we can learn to respond to our suffering by saying with the Apostle Paul:

Therefore we do not lose heart. Though outwardly we are wasting away, yet inwardly we are being renewed day by day. For our light and momentary troubles are achieving for us an eternal glory that far outweighs them all. So we fix our eyes not on what is seen, but on what is unseen. For what is seen is temporary, but what is unseen is eternal (2 Corinthians 4:16-18).

Christ, our eternal King, our risen Lord and Savior, actually is in our midst with his angels. We may not connect with him, we may not even have a thought about him, but, nonetheless, always he is literally present in Spirit and is ready to care for us and help us – if only we will reach out for his hand of grace. And if we didn't know how to do that in the past then with the Lord who was, is, and is to come and we can go back into our memory and our heart and seek his healing.

Jesus didn't leave us as orphans, but gave us his Spirit – the Strengthener, the gift of the Father – to be with us and in us no matter what (John 14:16-18, Acts 1:4). One of the most touching ways that he told us this was in his teaching that each child (and by extension any person who is child-like) has angels in the heavens (which come down to the air we breathe) that are always beholding for him or her, you or me, the face of the Father who is in the heavens (Matthew 18:10).

God is near! God's kingdom is here! O to be as child trusting in our Heavenly Father!

It's very helpful if we understand and trust in the immediate reality of God's kingdom of love *before* we find ourselves in suffering. Because once painful circumstances hit us we'll tend to react according to what we already believe and what habits we've formed.

A Girl Dying of Leukemia Trusted Jesus
A physician named Daniel Foster tells a remarkable, true story about a precious little girl who trusted Jesus in her suffering and found peace. The girls' mother was very distressed and asked Dr. Foster why one of her twin girls

was dying of leukemia and the other was not. He tried to help her find comfort in God, but she was agnostic. So he gave her C.S. Lewis' book *The Problem of Pain* to read, but after reading it she said, "Why did you give me this B.S. to read?"

But the young mother had a dramatic paradigm shift after an experience with her daughter. This girl had never been taken to church or Sunday school and had never been told about Jesus Christ. As she lay dying, suddenly she turned to her mother sitting by the bed and said, "Mother, who is Jesus?"

And the mother replied, "He was a great man, a wonderful teacher."

The little girl asked, "Do you like Him, mother?"

And she replied, "Yes, I like Him very much."

Some time later the little girl spoke again, "Do you see Him, mother?"

"See who?" the mother replied.

And the little girl said, "Jesus. He is standing at the foot of the bed. Do you see His crown, mother?"

She replied, "No, honey, I can't see it."

Then the little girl said, "He is calling for me, mother." And with that she died.

The girl's mother and the nurse who were present reported that this happened at dawn on a very calm day and at the moment when the little girl died there was *a sudden great rush of wind* heard outside the house and then it turned calm again.

After the risen Christ appeared to her dying daughter the mother became a Christian and joined Dr. Foster's church.[35]

The God Jesus Knows as "Abba"
If it weren't for Jesus we wouldn't know that God is our Abba. Perhaps we wouldn't even know God as Father, as there are only a few references about this in the Old Testament. Thankfully, Jesus not only spoke of God as a loving Father and taught us to pray to him, "Our Father," but he demonstrated the tender and affectionate Abba Father heart of God. And because of this our New Testament is full of inspiring and healing verses on the Father's love for us.[36]

"Abba" is one of our most precious names for God. It is maybe the best name for describing the heart of God. Abba is the Hebrew word for "Papa" or "Da-da," the very first words that come from the mouth of a little Jewish boy or girl. It ought to bring a smile to our face and warm our

---

[35] Dr. Foster was the head of internal medicine at the Southwestern Medical School in the University of Texas. He told this story in a lecture he gave at First Presbyterian Church of Dallas, Texas in 1999. http://www.firstpresdallas.org/

[36] See "The Father Loves You!", a compilation of Bible verses, at SoulShepherding.org.

hearts to pray to God as Abba. It did for Jesus. Probably he often talked with God as Abba.

We know that in Jesus' time of great need in the Garden of Gethsemane, just before he went to the cross for us, he cried out to God again and again as his "Abba" (Mark 14:36). When Jesus was in anguish he trusted his Abba like a little boy. He is showing us here and throughout the Gospels, and the Apostle Paul elaborates on this, that God desires for us to know him as our Abba (Romans 8:15, Galatians 4:6). The significance of this is hard to put in words...

The One who is the Lord Almighty, the King of kings... The One who is the Creator of the heavens, the earth, and you and I... The One who flung the stars in the sky and calls them each by name... The One who makes the clouds his chariot and whose voice is like the sound of thunder... The One to whom all the angels in heaven bow as they sing, "Holy! Holy! Holy! Is the God who was, who is, and who is to come." The One who shines like the sun and is so awesome and glorious that whenever anyone in the Bible encounters him in a vision or hears him speak they fall to the ground trembling, completely undone... *This Sovereign Lord God* says to you and I: "You can call me 'Da-da.'"

Da-da. God wants us to know that the youngest, most vulnerable, most needy part of you and I is welcome in his arms. He wants us to find safe refuge in his loving embrace. Because he knows that in order for us to live in his abundant life and to share this life effectively with others we need to trust him.

Jesus and the Children
Jesus showed us the Abba Father love of God especially in the way he treated children:

[Jesus and his disciples] came to Capernaum. When he was in the house, he asked them, "What were you arguing about on the road?" But they kept quiet because on the way they had argued about who was the greatest.

Sitting down, Jesus called the Twelve and said, "If anyone wants to be first, he must be the very last, and the servant of all."

He took a little child and had him stand among them. Taking him in his arms, he said to them, "Whoever welcomes one of these little children in my name welcomes me; and whoever welcomes me does not welcome me but the one who sent me" (Mark 9:33-37)

Now watch what happens just a few days after Jesus taught his disciples this lesson that to be truly great they need to welcome children as a way of welcoming him:

People were bringing little children to Jesus to have him touch them, but the disciples rebuked them. When Jesus saw this, he was indignant. He said to them, "Let the little children come to me, and do not hinder them, for the kingdom of God belongs to such as these. I tell you the truth, anyone who will not receive the kingdom of God like a little child will never enter it." And he took the children in his arms, put his hands on them and blessed them. (Mark 10:13-16).

The disciples could've helped these children to connect with Jesus. They could've played with them, listened to them, told them a story, cared for them. They had seen Jesus care for children and they had heard him stress that they needed to do the same. But there they were shooing the children away as if they were a nuisance, as if Jesus was too busy with more important things to make time for children. By rejecting the children they rejected Jesus! (Matthew 25:40, Luke 9:48).

So Jesus rebuked his disciples again and went farther to drive his point home to them, telling them that not only were they putting off him when they put off the children, but also they were closing the door to God's kingdom for themselves! He insisted that they had to learn to trust him like little children if they wanted to participate in the reality of his kingdom. This was a shocking teaching to them! In their day people viewed children as possessions. Even in our socially advanced society it wasn't long ago that we said with impatience, "Children are to be seen, not heard."

But Jesus says for everyone to hear and with his arms open: "Bring the little children to me!" He cuddled with them, played with them, and loved on them. Jesus was sharing with the children (and adults like you and me!) the love of his Abba that he experienced. Brennan Manning, an author beloved by hurting people who are seeking God[37], writes to draw us closer to the God that Jesus knew personally as Abba:

---

[37] Brennan Manning is a friar and priest, appreciated as much by evangelicals as Catholics. He struggled with alcoholism and depression in his life, which drove him deeper in his love-relationship with Jesus

It can be unequivocally stated that the central, most important theme in the personal life of Jesus, the theme that lies at the very heart of the revelation that he is, is his growing trust, intimacy and love of his Abba, his heavenly Father. The interior life of Christ was completely Father-centered. The master clue for interpreting the gospel narrative, the foundation of Jesus' compelling demands, the source of his towering zeal was his personal experience of God as Abba.[38]

Jessica Trusted God as her Abba

Jessica's mother didn't believe her story about her father abusing her. She felt she was alone with her "dirty secret" until she took courage and told me everything.

I believed Jessica. I spent many hours listening to Jessica cry, question, scream, or be completely unable to speak. I sat with her week after week as she trembled, hid her face in her hands, and told her story, little-by-little. It was a long healing process for her. She had many losses to grieve. She needed to be healed of shame. She needed to recover her dignity, her voice, and her ability to say no. She needed to learn to forgive and trust again.

For a long time Jessica couldn't "forgive" God. Her image of God was damaged and distorted. God is a Father and fathers – men in general – were not to be trusted. She saw

---

and his Abba and gave him tremendous compassion for the hurts of other people.

[38] Brennan Manning, *Stranger to Self-Hatred* (Dimension Books: 1982), p. 40.

the compassion of Jesus in the Gospels and she trusted him, but she didn't know how to see him as active in her life, because she couldn't find him in the pain of her childhood.

Learning to trust me, a man, as her therapist and then looking to me as Christ's Ambassador to her helped Jessica heal her image of God. Prayerful meditation on Scriptures also helped, like Psalm 91 that presents God as a loving mother and Jesus' Parable of the Prodigal Son that gives an amazing picture of God as a Father who is compassionate, generous, and sacrificial.

And healing of memory prayer was important for Jessica. She learned how to take the hand of the frozen mute little girl who felt so bad about herself and lead her to Jesus and through him to trust God as her Abba.

Embracing Abba
Like Jessica, to trust God as your Abba you need to approach him from the posture of the child inside of you. This is where growing up in Christ begins (Ephesians 4:22, 1 Peter 2:2). If you've internalized "Don't be needy or emotional" then it may be difficult for you to access the child-like part of you. You may have lost touch with it long ago, but I promise you that there is a little boy or a little girl inside of you still today. And probably he or she is similar to what you were like as a child. The hurts or inhibitions or bad feelings that you had then you may still have deep in your heart.

When you think about the child part of you maybe like me you relate to the children in the Gospel story who needed Jesus' blessing but had difficulty getting to him. When you were a child there may have been some important adults in your life who didn't welcome you into Jesus' arms.

Perhaps like Jessica you were mistreated by a parent or other caregiver in some hurtful ways. Or maybe the adults you depended on loved you in that they protected you and provided for you and wanted the best for you and never would've abused you, but they did not listen to your heart and embrace you in compassion. Or it may be that a parent was depressed or had an addiction or there was some other painful dysfunction in your family.

When you were little your parents and teachers represented God to you even if they weren't Christians. If they were patient, compassionate, and helpful then this encouraged you to trust and connect with God. If they were preoccupied, critical, or detached then this probably damaged your heart connection to you Heavenly Father.

Be careful not to deny or minimize whatever hurts or unmet needs or other issues of mistrust that you have in your past, but to bring them to Jesus and to Abba Father for the ministry of his healing love. We need to help one another with to establish a deeper trust in God so that we can become more of the persons that he has created us to be.

Spiritual Exercise: Be Playful
Tragically, many people when they imagine the face of God they see a solemn face, or worse a frown. They don't see God' smile. And when they think about what it means to be a Christian joyful play is the farthest thing from their minds. They don't really know Jesus.

Jesus showed us that playfulness is at the center of his kingdom of the heavens! He enjoyed playing with children; He blessed babies and he cuddled with kids. He delighted so much in the ways of children that, in sharp contrast to the culture of his time, he held them up as role models. Meditating on the fun, playful, and humorous aspects of Jesus in the Gospels helps me to be freer to be like a child with him – it helps me to cultivate the affectionate attitude of counting the seconds to be with my Abba. Being very serious, determined, and hard-working by nature this has been a great blessing for me!

To grow spiritually we need to set aside times to play! If you're a serious person by nature than you may not like me saying this. It may seem to you like a ridiculous oxymoron for me to say that *play is a spiritual discipline.* But before you dismiss me as being silly or just plain wrong, open your heart to God and consider if he might have something for you here. The truth is that generally it is best for you if a playful attitude permeates *all* that you say and do, including the spiritual disciplines that you practice.[39]

Playful? What does this mean? To be playful is more than playing games! It's doing something you love to do with someone you love to be with; it's going on an adventure; it's being spontaneous and creative; it's having fun in the

---

[39] Richard Foster gave what many people think of as on oxymoron title to his book: *The Celebration of Discipline.* Most people don't put the words "celebration" and "discipline" together and this is the brilliance of his groundbreaking work. He teaches that we need to bring a grace-permeated and celebratory attitude to all of our spiritual disciplines (Harper & Row: 1978).

moment and not taking things too seriously; it's being willing to be messy as part of the fun; it's being ready to discover something new; it's laughing about the humor in something; it's delighting in all that God provides for your enjoyment.

When we play with Jesus it helps us to de-stress, lighten up, smile, and slip right into his easy yoke.

The Playfulness of Jesus
The Gospels give us many examples of Jesus' child-like playfulness and fun-loving nature bubbling out from him…
Turning water to wine so the dancing at the wedding could continue
Explaining to people that they're worth more to the Father than two sparrows
Telling people who were worried about what they were going to wear to look at how the wildflowers were dressed
Winking at the Greek woman as he told her and his disciples that he couldn't heal her daughter because he couldn't give the children's bread to a "dog" like her and then healing her anyway
Sending demons out from a man and into a herd of pigs who then stampeded off a cliff!
Walking on the water at night right passed his disciples as they rowed in their boat in a storm
Telling Peter to pay their taxes by finding a coin in the mouth of the first fish he caught
Prodding Zacchaeus to jump down from the tree he was hiding in so they could have dinner together
Going to parties with his societies' outcasts
Calling the Pharisees "white washed tombstones"
Calling out to God as his "Abba" (Hebrew for "Papa" or "Daddy")

Walking right through a locked door to show his scared apostles that he indeed had risen from the dead
Telling his disciples who had fished all night and caught nothing simply to throw their nets to the other side of the boat and then providing for them a huge haul of fish that broke their nets

Jesus is showing us that in the Kingdom of the Heavens music "plays," lambs and calves skip along, birds sing, children and the child-like dance, new wine flows, and people talk and laugh at the banquet table. Why? Because, "How great is the love the Father has lavished on us that we should be called children of God!" (1 John 3:1).

It's Time to Play with Jesus!
As a child I remember knocking on the door of a neighbor friend and asking, "Can you play?" I always felt like a risk. I was being vulnerable – I knew he might say no. But usually he said yes and that little question from my heart led to games of catch, fishing expeditions, walking to 7-11 to get a Slurpee, messing around by the train tracks, catching frogs, and all kinds of fun!

This week pick a time to say to Jesus, "Can you play?" Ask Abba to help you to set aside time to stop your serious work and to relax and have fun with Jesus. Pray to be set free of your inhibitions and melancholies and to be playful, even silly! Pray that Jesus would minister Abba's healing love to you to help you know that the child-like part of you is good, loveable and loving, delightful, fun, creative.

Let's each of do a little experiment this week that will help us to play with Jesus. This will be fun – *serious* fun!

It's important that we *enjoy* our life with Jesus in his kingdom – it helps us to grow in our trust in God as our loving Father. It may stretch you to do this exercise, but if you don't try new things you can't grow spiritually. And besides, the child from your history and the one in your heart knows how to play – we just need to tap into that.

This week pick one of my spiritual experiments to try out as way of expressing the child in you and connecting with Jesus and his Abba. I've done each one of these and I promise that if you put your heart into doing one of these experiments that it'll help to deep your trust in God:

Find a sidewalk or a long hallway and start skipping as you say, "I am the disciple Jesus loves! I am the disciple Jesus loves!" It'll make you happy. It'll make you feel like a child. This is a way of using your body to engage your mind and heart in being God's child. (It's okay to do this exercise where no one can see you!)

Sing songs of thanks and praise to God (in church or by yourself) and use your hands to express your worship (using your hands will help to express your love for God with thoughtfulness and affection). Make up your own hand motions like kids are taught to do in Sunday School.

Go onto the Internet to find a picture of Jesus laughing or playing with children. Sit on the floor (little children are on the floor a lot!) and imagine being a child and enjoying Jesus. Smile – better yet, *laugh!* – with Jesus.

Go to a beach and draw a huge heart in the sand and write in it, "I love Jesus!" Or you can do this with chalk on your driveway or back patio.

Color a picture to express your desire to be free and child-like in your love for God as your Abba.

Breath Prayer
The playfulness of Jesus is a testimony of God's love for children. And it's validation that there is a little and vulnerable part of you that longs for your Heavenly Father to lift you up in his arms with joy! To be free to play and laugh, express your needs, love and be loved. Have you brought this child in you to Jesus and his Abba? Does your heart cry out to God with affection and delight, "Abba! Papa!"

There is a void in you and in me that only Abba's love can fill. But we cling to people. We try to impress people. We rush around and strive to succeed. We worry. We accumulate more and more stuff. We live for new, exciting experiences. We escape into entertainments or alcohol.

O, my friends, Jesus shows us the Abba Father love of God that we yearn for! Being embraced by Abba is the treasure of the Kingdom of God. Nothing else will satisfy our souls.

I was reminded of my longing for Abba during a time of extended silence and solitude on an "Embracing Abba" retreat that my wife Kristi and I helped to lead. As I walked through the gardens on a beautiful spring day I prayed a favorite Breath Prayer I learned years ago from going on retreat with Brennan Manning: "Abba... I belong to you."[40] As I thought about how I need Jesus to help me rely on

---

[40] Brennan Manning, *Abba's Child* (Navpress: 1994).

Abba's love a new prayer came to me: "Jesus... Embrace me in Abba's love."

What a blessing it was to me! I prayed it over and over, very slowly and deeply. I did it as a Breath Prayer. I breathed in deep with a smile: "Jesus..."

I breathed out, still smiling, "Embrace me in Abba's love."

That little prayer kept me in Abba's arms for hours. I prayed about other things too, but I kept coming back to my yearning for my Abba.

And to help me get more in touch with the child in me I got out crayons and colored a picture of my longing to be embraced by Jesus and his Abba. (Maybe it would help you to draw a picture of your relationship with your Abba?) And I reflected on how my life would be different if I were *really free to live as Abba's child always.*

Try imagining yourself as one of the children in this Gospel story. See yourself as a child. Picture what you looked like when you were little and what your personality was like...

When you were a child who helped to connect you with Jesus and his Abba? Perhaps a memory comes to mind for you to thank God for...

Who made it harder for you to see and trust God as a loving Father? (Sometimes the same people in some ways helped our image of God and in other ways hurt it.) Perhaps a memory comes to mind for you to pray for God to heal...

How do you feel about your child-like self *today?* Here are some questions that may help you to understand how you really feel about your inner child...
How do you feel about being vulnerable and needy?
Are you comfortable being playful, even silly?
What do you say to yourself when you make a mistake?

Ask Jesus to help you talk to Abba about the child in you and to embrace him freely. See Jesus smiling with his arms open to you... He shows you that God is your loving Abba... Take a deep breath... Relax in the arms of Jesus, your Lord and Savior... Trust your Abba...

"Jesus... Embrace me in Abba's love."

Use this little prayer to help you this week and to practice God's presence.

Salty Questions
As spiritual friends or as a small group this is our opportunity to help one another to grow in our trust in God as our Abba Father, by being real and vulnerable in our conversation, to bring out the child-like part of us. When we share our hurts, longings, or the precious things that Christ is teaching us it is salty – it makes others thirsty for more of God, adds God-flavor to life, and preserves the grace and wisdom that God has been dispensing.

What is one thing that you learned about trusting your Heavenly Father and his kingdom?

What aspect of God's love is hardest for you to trust? What is an example?

What helps you to be child-like before God? For instance, how did it affect you to pray, "Jesus... Embrace me in Abba's love"?

You Can Live in Jesus' Easy Yoke: Lesson #4
Think God's Thoughts about You

Twenty-five years ago when I was studying to become a psychologist I had to practice leading counseling sessions in front of a one-way mirror. Behind the mirror was my professor, who was holding a clipboard to make notes on how well I offered empathy, made interpretations, and was helpful to the client. Huddled around the master counselor was my whole class of graduate students in training. *Everyone was watching me!*

The client was an 18-year old young woman just starting out as a freshman in college. It had to be difficult for her to share her life story and emotional struggle with a "rookie" counselor and to do so in front of a whole class of onlookers! (That was the price she paid for a free therapy session.) But I was so anxious about having *my* performance scrutinized that I had trouble tuning into her feelings – it's no wonder I didn't get very good marks from my professor!

When my professor gave me "constructive criticism" in front of my peers (so they could learn at the same time) it was embarrassing. I felt like an awful therapist. My head dropped and my shoulders drooped as I thought to myself, *Who are you kidding? You don't even know how to show good empathy, let alone guide the counseling session in a helpful way. Why are you wasting the best years of your life and tens of thousands of dollars to get a Ph.D.? Just give it up. Surely, you misunderstood God's calling on your life and he has something else for you to do.*

Thankfully, I got help with my self-criticalness and I didn't quit studying to become a psychologist. So for almost twenty-five years now I've been blessed to live out 2 Corinthians 5:20, my Life Verse, serving as "Christ's Ambassador" to people who are hurting or struggling. To get free of self-criticism I had to *change classrooms:* I walked out of the one-way mirror room and into Christ's room. With Jesus as my teacher, instead of harsh people or my own internal critic, truth and grace worked together for my healing (John 1:14, 17).

"I'm Not a Good Enough Christian"
I have since learned that I am not the only one who has lived in front of a one-way mirror being watched by a critic! Many people I talk with suffer from self-condemnation, like my wife Kristi. I am just one of countless people who admire Kristi as beautiful, wise, compassionate, and very capable in so many areas. She is an incredible wife, mother, psychotherapist, and co-founder with me of our *Soul Shepherding* ministry to pastors, leaders, and caregivers. For twenty-five years I have appreciated her as the loveliest servant of Christ on earth! And yet until recent years she was frequently overcome with self-hatred.

For instance, as we were raising up our three children (who are now each in high school or college – wow, those years went fast!) Kristi often felt bad about herself as a mother. She compared herself to other Orange County, CA moms and felt inadequate. Kristi would tell me things like, "I don't fit in with the women at the kids' school or at church. They're so attractive, intelligent, and generous. It's no wonder they don't invite me to things and don't really want to know me.

"I hear about other moms taking their kids to music lessons, soccer, and scouts and I feel bad that I only let our kids be in one activity at a time – *that's all I can manage!* But look at Joanne – she does all those things for her kids and she does such an amazing job of leading the Awanas program at church. Recently she had all the kids over to her house. She served them healthy snacks and made it so fun for everyone. She got them in groups by their teams and she helped them make the cutest team banners that I've ever seen. Each team picked a Bible verse and each child made a felt doll of themselves with yarn hair and eyes that matched theirs, team uniforms, and a little piece of sports equipment – even the boys enjoyed doing it.

"I can't do that! I'm not that creative and organized. I just don't have the energy. I'm overwhelmed with just taking care of our three kids, the house, and working part time. Some days I'm doing good just to get out of bed and make it through another day!"

I feel sad remembering how inadequate and discouraged Kristi felt back then, but even worse than that were the times that she *plummeted into self-hatred:* "I'll never be good enough!" she cried out from her quicksand. "I need to be better and to do more, especially as a mother, but I'm just weak and lazy. My kids are suffering because I'm not doing enough for them. And the worst part is that I've let God down; I'm disappointing him. I'm not a good Christian and I'm sure not a good witness for Christ. I'm afraid that I'm burying my talent and God is angry with me, but I don't feel like I even have a talent."

How is Your Self-Esteem?

Most people I talk with struggle with self-criticism to some extent. Some are vulnerable to being besieged by feelings of guilt and shame. How about you? What is your concept of yourself? Try my survey to help you better understand how you view yourself. Answer each question below with "yes" (mostly true for you) or "no" (mostly *not* true for you). Then circle each "yes" answer:

When I look in the mirror I tend to focus on my faults.
When I do a job I usually think I should have done it better.
I do not feel I have much to offer to other people.
I feel guilty about sins from my past.
I often compare myself to other people and come up short.
When I speak in front of people I am self-critical.
I often worry that other people think badly of me.
When I make mistake I tend to get frustrated with myself.
I do not feel that I have much to be proud of.
I get frustrated about my weaknesses.
When I do not succeed at something I feel inadequate.
When I have a conflict with someone I feel it is my fault.
When someone shows me positive attention I feel unworthy.
I think more about my negative traits than my positive ones.
I often criticize myself.
There are things that I do not like about myself.
When someone is angry with me I feel bad about myself.
I do not like myself when I get emotional.
If you have five or more yes answers (or you have any yes answers that are quite painful for you) then probably you need help learning to appreciate your belovedness.

Worm Theology

How did your survey come out? Do you struggle with feeling bad about yourself? If so then when someone criticizes you it can be devastating and demoralizing because *it's two against none!* Your own internal critic and the observer behind the one-way mirror are ganging up on you. To make matters worse your condemning self-evaluations may be "baptized" by misinterpretations of Scripture.

Many Christians who struggle with self-condemnation have a "worm theology." They believe that the Bible teaches them to think of themselves as worms. They feel eligible, even deserving, of being talked down because they accept negative messages like:
"I'm not significant" (or "I'm not beautiful")
"It's prideful to think highly of yourself"
"My heart is wicked and deceitful" (or "I'm just a sinner saved by grace")
"I should feel guilty"
"I messed up so I have to make up for it"

These negative messages are a heavy, painful yoke to bear! They evoke anxiety, guilt, and shame. Careful Bible study shows that they are false narratives. *God does not want to condemn you – he wants to extend mercy to you!* Christians who view God as devaluing or condemning them are projecting onto God their own self-criticisms, which originated from being wounded by people they relied on. Self-condemnations are facilitated by Satan, the father of lies (John 8:44) and accuser of God's people (Revelation 12:10).

Worm theology is not Biblical. When the Psalmist cries out, "I am a worm and not a man!" (Psalm 22:6) he is not giving a theological statement on the nature of people, but is describing his personal feelings of humiliation over being persecuted. When Jeremiah writes the word of the Lord that, "The heart is deceitful above all things and beyond cure," he is not describing the hearts of those who love the Lord, but is referring to the hearts of people who are separated from God's saving grace (Jeremiah 17:9). When Paul teaches, "I know that in me (that is, in my flesh,) dwells no good thing" he is contrasting his natural self (his "flesh" or old self) that is corrupted by separation from God with his Christ-redeemed self (his new and true self) that relies on the Holy Spirit (Romans 7:18, KJV). We need to watch out for these "Biblical Blunders that Bruise and Confuse!"[41]

We Need More than Self-Love

Our typical Christian answer to low self-esteem is something like: "You are special to God so believe his affirmations of you in the Bible and love yourself. He created you wonderfully so appreciate all the good things about your personality and abilities. He's given you gifts so use them to accomplish great things."

Indeed the Bible is full of wonderful affirmations of how greatly God loves us and treasures us! Here are just a few examples (more to come later!):

---

[41] These are just a few examples from my list of "Biblical Blunders that Bruise and Confuse." See SoulShepherding.org.

"Therefore, there is now no condemnation for those who are in Christ Jesus" (Romans 8:1). This means that even when you sin God does not want you stuck feeling guilty – he wants to feel sad because you're missing out and he calls you to you run into his arms for mercy and healing.[42]

"For we are God's masterpiece. He has created us anew in Christ Jesus, so we can do the good things he planned for us long ago" (Ephesians 2:10, NLT). Believe it – you are God's *masterpiece!* This verse can also be translated as, "You are God's beautifully written poem to deliver his message in a unique and delightful way!"

"The LORD your God is with you, he is mighty to save. He will take great delight in you, he will quiet you with his love, he will rejoice over you with singing" (Zephaniah 3:17). Imagine it: God delighting over you as a father delights over his precious little child, he sings a love song over you to calm you down and put you to sleep!

Sadly, you and I are prone to misuse God's promises and therefore miss out on the good that God intends to get to us and *get through us to other people.* The subtle problem here is that we readily become *self-absorbed* in our efforts to feel more valuable and to be self-actualized. If we're not careful we end up committed to a "self-help" project of trying to raise our own self-esteem (or get God to do it for us) by believing the right Bible verses or going to the

---

[42] See 2 Corinthians 7:10-11 for Paul's differentiation of "wordly sorrow" (guilt, condemnation, shame) that leads to isolation and death and "godly sorrow" (conviction, sadness) that leads to repentance and life. God never wants you in the state of worldly sorrow – it doesn't do any good for you or anyone else.

right church program or joining the right support group. As we said earlier that is a consumer-oriented Christianity that actually works against Jesus' gospel of the kingdom of God.

Jesus warned not only his serious students but also *the curious crowds* against pursuing a self-help strategy for improving their lives:

Calling the crowd to join his disciples, [Jesus] said, "Anyone who intends to come with me has to let me lead. You're not in the driver's seat; I am. Don't run from suffering; embrace it. Follow me and I'll show you how. Self-help is no help at all. Self-sacrifice is the way, my way, to saving yourself, your true self. What good would it do to get everything you want and lose you, the real you? What could you ever trade your soul for? (Mark 8:34-37).[43]

There is no doubt that *God delights to bless us in every way,* but Jesus – and the whole Bible for that matter – shows us a different approach to self-esteem. The Bible directs us to focus not on self, but on God. Proper self-love is a natural byproduct of loving God. But when we go directly after self-esteem and "claim" it for ourselves from one of God's promises then we're in danger of invalidating the promise because we're not in the right posture to

---

[43] As we saw in Jesus' beatitudes his Gospel message is an *inversion* of the world's way: Again and again he said things like, "The last shall be first and the first shall be last" (Matthew 20:16; see also Matthew 19:30 and Mark 9:35), "The greatest among you will be your servant" (Matthew 23:11; see also Matthew 20:26), and "Whoever exalts himself will be humbled, and whoever humbles himself will be exalted" (Matthew 23:12).

make use of it. *The wonderful blessings that the Bible offers are always associated with living in submission to God's kingdom rule.* We can't make them come true for ourselves.

Jesus' easy yoke is a *yoke.* We don't get his "easy" without his "yoke," the two go together. His yoke *binds* us to his leadership, his work, his way, and in time we discover that being in the Lord's yoke as his apprentice is the best and most blessed life possible! It is from inside the yoke that we're finally able to rest in God's love which has been there for us all along. It is in this posture of submission to God that the Psalmist marvels, "The glorious Lord Almighty is mindful of me! He cares for me! He crowns me with his glory! Everywhere I go he is there thinking of me with concern and saying that I am precious to him."[44] And Jesus elaborated on this, indicating that the Father's care of us is so intimate that he even counts the hairs on our heads! (Matthew 10:30). There is no doubt: God is thinking of you with love *right now!*

Delighting in the Lord who Delights in You!
Yes, in love God is thinking of you, but *are you thinking of God?* The Lord is delighting in you, but *are you delighting in the Lord?* This is critical question. We need to pause and reflect on this: ask yourself, "Do I delight in the Lord? Do I thrill to connect with Christ?" The Bible teaches, "Delight yourself in the Lord and he will give you the desires of your heart" (Psalm 37:4). The true source of self-esteem is that when we love God (which includes loving others in his

---

[44] My paraphrases from Psalms 8:4-5 and 139:6-7, 17.

name) *we are loving the One who is Love and so we find ourselves cherished by him.*

But if you're not appreciating God then his love won't very well get through to you. Jesus could be in the flesh beside you showering you with his kindness and mercy, but if you're not looking at him, listening to him, and trusting him then it won't do you any good. This is the problem that many of us have: we're thinking so much about our deficiencies or what we should be doing to solve our problems that we miss the opportunity to think about God and the beautiful things he is already doing in our lives. In other words, if we haven't gotten rid of our internal critic then it'll deflect the grace-messages that God communicates to us. How tragic it is when our own harsh self-judgments and unrealistic self-expectations render God's love for us ineffective!

As Paul taught, "Those who trust God's action in them find that God's Spirit is in them – living and breathing God! Obsession with self in these matters is a dead end; attention to God leads us out into the open, into a spacious, free life" (Romans 8:6-7, MSG). Being self-critical is a form of anxious obsession on self. We need to take the internal critic off the throne of our heart and adore the God of grace!

Worship is the most important thing we can do. Ray Ortlund taught me to make enthusiastic worship of the Lord my number one priority in life. (After all, it's the first of the Ten Commandments that God gave us!) I spent hundreds of hours talking with Ray in small group, on retreat, and over many private lunches and in every single conversation I found myself drawn to delight more in God and give more of myself to serve him. Ray explained:

Worship is the highest and noblest act that any person can do. When [people] worship, God is satisfied!... And when you worship, you are fulfilled!... We who were once self-centered have to be completely changed so that we can shift our attention outside of ourselves and become able to worship Him...

Worship is top priority. Everything, absolutely everything, must be set aside to do this...

A person may say, "Well, I just don't get anything out of it."

You get nothing out of it?! You get nothing out of the Word of the eternal God?! You get nothing out of the great hymns of the church?! You get nothing out of prayer through Jesus Christ to God Almighty?!

That's because you don't know how to put anything into it. It shows our deep misunderstanding of what worship is all about... Worship is the meaning of the whole thing of living.[45]

To worship God all we need to do is to put our minds on him. We readily become God-absorbed when we meditate on Scripture or the wonders of creation. God's goodness and beauty naturally draw us in to give thanks to him, sing his praises, devote our lives to him, and love our neighbor

---

[45] Ray Ortlund, *Lord Make My Life a Miracle* (Regal Books:1974), p. 40.

in Jesus' name. What joy is ours when we think deeply on the Lord! Returning to Ray's words again,

God alone is the balanced Person. God the Father, God the Son, God the Holy Spirit – they alone are really whole. God alone is sufficient in Himself. We have been so constructed as His people that we are only whole, we are only sufficient when all our lives are revolving around Him. We must be God-centered![46]

And when we are God-centered we start reflecting God's glory! "Those who look to him are radiant; their faces are never covered with shame" (Psalm 34:5).

Think on the Trinity

What joy it brings me to meditate on the Trinity! Father, Son, and Holy Spirit each are all-powerful and self-sustaining, enjoying fullness of life in their own selves. No member of the Trinity needs anything or has to answer to anybody, but will out of love each can choose to depend on or submit to one another or, within limits, to a lesser being. In other words, God is *humble.* Yes, the Lord Almighty is humble! The King of kings comes as a servant. Immanuel was born in a smelly barn, laid in an animal feeding trough, raised by a poor family in an tiny village, worked as an obscure carpenter, went into public ministry as a nomad, was rejected by friends and neighbors, and crucified as a criminal. The humility of God in Christ is perhaps the most stunning and winsome characteristic of God.

---

[46] Ray Ortlund, *Lord Make My Life a Miracle* (Regal Books:1974), p. 23.

Consider the other-centered way that members of the Godhead rejoice to relate to each other: Father, Son, and Spirit take turns shining the spotlight on one another. The Father sends us the gift of the Holy Spirit and Jesus breathes the Spirit into us. And the Spirit calls out in our hearts, "Papa Father!" and "Jesus is Lord." Back and forth they love and praise one another! The Father thunders from heaven, "Jesus is my beloved son and in him I am well pleased" and the Spirit lights on him in the form of a dove. And Jesus replies that the Father is the greatest and warns us never to speak a word against the Holy Spirit. This is incredible!

And the divine deference doesn't stop there. God stoops down to make *us* great! (Psalm 18:35). The Father shares his glory with us (John 17:22). The Lord Jesus comes with a towel to wash our feet (John 13:1-17). The Spirit that raised Jesus from the dead comes to live inside our souls (Romans 8:11). This is incredible (I know I keep saying that!). Isn't the Trinity so beautiful? Don't you feel inspired to join in their way of being? Sure enough, when we see and appreciate God's humble generosity it impels us to give up our self-centered ways and seek to be a blessing to others as the Trinity has been to us. So we shine the spotlight on God – more than that we worship him as God! – *and* we honor one another above ourselves.

You're Invited to *the Dance!*
Maybe you know the experience of not being invited to the Homecoming Dance? Or being one the last people picked for a team? It hurts to be left out. And when we experience this enough times we come to believe, *That's who I am – unwanted. I'm a reject.* Tragically, this belief becomes a self-fulfilling prophecy in which the person who

feels eligible to be rejected unwittingly finds judgmental or fickle people to befriend and unconsciously evokes rejection in relationships. It's a vicious cycle. Perhaps we've all experienced rejection somewhere in life and have had some feelings of being undesirable.

Listen: it is to *you,* my friend, that that Trinity says, "Come on in! Join our square dance!"

A square dance with the Trinity? Yes! Eugene Peterson's explanation of joining the fellowship of the Trinity! He says that in approaching the Trinity we need to visualize a square dance that we're invited to join. His vision, which goes back to fourth century monks, is that Father, Son, and Spirit are giving and responding to one another in a celebratory love dance that we're invited to join.[47] It is in this spirit that the Psalmist prays to God, "Oh, visit the earth, ask her to join the dance!... Surprise us with love at daybreak; then we'll skip and dance all the day long... Your revelation is the tune I dance to" (Psalm 65:9, 90:14, 119:77; all MSG). The Apostle Paul sees the dance too. He urges us, "Keep on doing what we told you to do to please God, not in a dogged religious plod, but in a living, spirited dance" (1 Thessalonians 4:1, MSG).

But notice Paul says that we tend to approach God in a *dogged religious plod!* I'm afraid I've often caught myself in a dogged religious plod! How about you? If you're prone to doing your devotions out of guilt or pressure, rather

---

[47] Eugene Peterson, *Christ Plays in Ten Thousand Places: A Conversation in Spiritual Theology* (William B. Eerdmans Publishing Co: 2005). "Perichoresis" is the Greek word for "dance around" that the ancients writers use to describe the Trinity.

than out of free choice, then you've done some dogged religious plodding and you need to be careful. Legalism is a bad yeast that works through all the dough of our souls. It is not good to read the Bible, say your prayers, go to church, or serve others by "shoulding" on yourself! If you're doing that it means you're too focused on yourself, and not enough focused on God. To get out of this trap you probably need to discipline yourself for awhile *not* to have a "quiet time" or do anything religious. Instead, you need just to cry out to God honestly along these lines: "Dear Father, I long to experience the easy yoke of Jesus, but it seems so far. I'm tired of trying so hard to be a good Christian and feeling so inadequate. I'm spiritually dry and I can't find your living waters. I need to know that you love me even when I'm not doing the things I should. O Jesus, show me your smile!"

In the metaphor of the dance if you've been doing the dogged religious plod when you're invited to dance with the Trinity then it's like you feel pressured to get all the dance steps and sequences and movements right. But you can't dance that way and even if you could it's no fun! (If you're good at doing the dogged religious plod then you can even ruin dancing!) Instead of trying to memorize dance routines and do each step "right" we need to step aside and watch the Father, Son, and Spirit dance. Or appreciate David in the Psalms or other Christ-followers dancing in "the joy of the Lord." This way we can get drawn into the spirit of the Trinity's shared celebration and join in with the beautiful flow of how they freely and easily move together in rhythms of love and joy. Then we can respond to Trinity's invitation to dance with them, following their lead, and learning as we go... and laughing at ourselves when we're slow to catch on!

Jesus is our dance instructor that teaches us to dance in "Father and Son intimacies," to delight with him, his Father, and the Holy Spirit in the "unforced rhythms of grace" (Matthew 11: 27, 29, MSG). Have you ever thought of being yoked to an ox and pulling a plow across a field as being like dancing? I imagine not! What a beautiful picture Jesus gives us of what's like to do our daily activities in his easy yoke! What a glorious fulfillment of the ancient words of the Church father St. Irenaeus[48]: "The glory of God is man fully alive." Indeed, if we learn from Jesus to dance with the Trinity then we'll be dynamic witnesses for Christ because as Peter said people will ask us, "What is it in your life that makes you so alive?" (1 Peter 3:15, paraphrase).

In Christ

To follow Jesus into the Trinitarian dance we need to take into ourselves "the mind of Christ" (1 Corinthians 2:16). What would it be like if Jesus' mind lived in you and me? Surely this would mean that *his thoughts and his way of thinking would intermingle with our own and come to saturate our minds* so that it would eventually begin to be hard to distinguish our own thoughts from God's thoughts. Christ would be *in us.*

For instance, the way that we can take on the mind of Christ is to do what Jesus himself did and be formed by the words of Scripture. Jesus learned to pray from the Psalms and quoted Psalms many times (Luke 24:44). He realized his identity as Messiah by studying the prophecies of the

---

[48] St. Irenaeus (115 – 202) was bishop of Lugdunum in Gaul, which is now Lyons, France. He was a disciple of Polycarp, who himself was a disciple of John the Evangelist.

Old Testament (Luke 24:25-27). He got his life mission statement from the book of Isaiah (Luke 4:18-19, Isaiah 61:1-2). He continually said and did things "that the Scripture might be fulfilled."[49] He is the Word made flesh (John 1:14). To grow into having the mind of Christ at home in us – to think his thoughts about God, others, life, ourselves – we need to study carefully and meditate deeply on the Bible.

The Apostle Paul urged us, "Let the word of Christ dwell in your richly" (Colossians 3:16). Similarly, he prayed for us "that Christ will be more and more at home in your hearts as you trust in him" (Ephesians 3:17, NLT). He knew that receiving Christ into our heart-dwelling was the beginning of growing into God's way of abundant living. But he wanted us to grow even beyond receiving Christ *in me*. He showed us that Christ was welcoming us into *his home,* to live with him and in him, to live in his way and for his glory, to be a blessing to him and to other people in his name. We're invited to live *in Christ.*

In Christ. *In Christ!* O yes, to be in Christ!

Being in Christ is the key to life. Again and again the Apostle Paul implores us to live in Christ, which is to say in effect, "devote yourself to living as Jesus' apprentice." He lives this way himself, boasting, "I glory in Christ" (Romans 5:17). In fact, in his epistles he refers to our position "in Christ," 160 times![50] He says it again and again and again.

---

[49] Matthew 26:54, Mark 14:49, Luke 4:21, John 17:12, 19:24,28, 36.

[50] This also includes when Paul uses the wording "in him" or "in the Lord" to refer to our position "in Christ."

For instance, in Christ...

- We are a new creation (2 Corinthians 5:17)
- We become God's children (Galatians 3:26)
- We have every spiritual blessing (Ephesians 1:3)
- We have the forgiveness of sins (Ephesians 1:7)
- We have glorious riches (Philippians 4:19)
- We are rooted and built up (Colossians 2:7)
- We gain an excellent standing and great assurance (1 Timothy 3:13)

I want to be *in Christ!* I want him to be my "first love" (Revelation 2:4), "the center of [my] life" (Philippians 4:7, MSG), the "one thing I ask" (Psalm 27:4). I want to sit at his feet and bless him as Mary of Bethany did (John 12:1-8). I want to give up all things to follow him alone (Luke 9:24). I want to give him that drink of water he's thirsty for (John 4:7). Don't you want to respond to his invitation? Yes, of course, you do! You want to be at home in Christ more than anything else in the whole world. That's why you're in this *Easy Yoke* group!

Oh, to center our souls in Christ, opening up the depths of our being to rely on him above all and in all. He's our Fountainhead who spouts forth "a spring of water welling up to eternal life" (John 4:14) so that the Holy Spirit's "streams of living water will flow from within" us and out to the thirsty souls around us (John 7:38). Oh, to center ourselves in Christ, giving up all other identities, ideal selves, masks, and false selves. He's our Potter and we're the clay he molds to be useful for his glorious purposes (Isaiah 64:8). Oh, to center our lives in Christ, giving up all the self-propping-up distractions of materialism, dressing for attention, and striving to be the best. He's the Lord, our Maker, and we're his creatures who bow down to worship and adore him alone (Psalm 95:6). Oh, to live simply, free of bright lights, clutter, and distraction. He's the Good Shepherd and we're the humble sheep in his pasture (Psalm 100:3).

To be centered in Christ is our way to *life!* Dallas Willard explains:

> Those "in Christ" – that is, caught up in his life, in what he's doing, by the inward gift of birth from above "are of a new making, the old stuff no longer matters. It is the new that counts" (2 Corinthians 5:17, DW Paraphrase). Here in this new creation is the radical goodness that alone can thoroughly renovate the heart.[51]

Saved From Self-Hatred

It is the easy yoke life in Christ – the dance of life with the Trinity – that saves us from self-hatred. Kristi has grown in this life and found healing from guilt and shame. How did she get rid of the condemning judge in her head and rely on the grace of the Lord instead? What can we learn from her story?

Kristi followed the same advice that we tell the people we counsel and mentor: "You'll get help when you and I join God in caring for you." I like the way Aelred of Rievaulx (1110-1167)[52] said it many centuries ago:

---

[51] Dallas Willard, *Renovation of the Heart* (Navpress: 2002), p. 59.

[52] Aelred of Rievaulx was a Cistercian monk in the middle ages. At a time when friendship was viewed with caution in the Church, Aelred gave his heart to his friends and found Christ. He presents spiritual friendship as a special relationship that is both an expression of God's

Here we are, you and I, and I hope that Christ makes a third with us. No one can interrupt us now, no one can spoil our friendly conversation; no one's voice or noise will break in upon this pleasant solitude of ours. So come now, dearest friend, reveal your heart and speak your mind. You have a friendly audience; say whatever you wish. And let us not be ungrateful for this time or for our opportunity and leisure.[53]

Over time in her conversations with me, a counselor, a mentor, and her spiritual friends Kristi internalized the nonjudgmental love of God into her heart in new ways. By sharing herself honestly with people she felt safe with she took in God's grace deeper and deeper and displaced her internal critic. Like Kristi we all need a few Christ's Ambassadors in our lives to help us stay connected to the God of grace.

Kristi was surprised to learn that her self-condemnations were a form of pride or self-reliance; she had been cutting herself off from God by saying that she wasn't good enough to be loved by him, that his mercy wasn't enough for her. Unwittingly, she was diminishing her appreciation of God's greatness and hindering the flow of his grace and peace into her soul. Her self-focus left her in guilt and shame, powerless to effect her freedom.

---

love and a path to knowing God's love. His book is a journal record of intimate conversations he had with some of his friends.

[53] Aelred of Rievaulx, *Spiritual Friendship* (University of Scranton Press: 1994, originally published in 1157), p. 29.

Learning continually to re-direct her thoughts onto God was essential for Kristi. She needed something to hold onto so she wouldn't sink in the quicksand of self-deprecation: the Word of God became her solid lifeline. There are many ways she's been doing this: memorizing passages of Scripture like Romans 8 (see below), meditating on God's promises (like the ones above), and recalling to her mind how whenever anyone in the Bible asked the Lord for mercy he gave it.

For instance, Brennan Manning, one of Kristi's favorite authors, illustrated that Jesus is "the Deliverer from self-hatred through love" by healing Mary Magdalene from her shame and isolation:[54]

Magdalene was awed by the loveliness and compassion of this magnetic man. His eyes had called out to her, 'Come to me. Come now. Don't wait until you have your act cleaned up and your head on straight. Don't delay until you think you are properly disposed and free of pride and lust, jealousy and self-hatred. Come to me in your brokenness and sinfulness with your fears and insecurities and I will comfort you. I will come to you right where you are and love you just the way you are, just the way you are and not the way you think you should be.'

Jesus had convinced her that "winter had passed, that the rains were over and gone" (Song of Solomon 2:1), that her sins had been forgiven and that God now accepted her and approved of her. The moment she surrendered in faith,

---

[54] This beautiful, life transforming encounter that Mary Magdalene (we believe it was her, but aren't sure) had with Jesus is told in Luke 7:36-50.

love took effect and her life was transformed. The result was the inner healing of her heart manifested as peace, joy, gratitude and love... The creative power of Jesus' love called Magdalene to regard herself as He did, to see in herself the possibilities which he saw in her.[55]

Manning says that like Mary Magdalene you and I cannot heal ourselves from our self-hatred, our anxiety, or any of our problems:

I cannot free myself. I must be set free. Jesus... invites me to make friends with my insecurities, smile at them, outgrow them in patient endurance, live with the serene confidence that he never abandons his friends, even when we disappoint him...

Jesus says: that is the way my Father is. He wants you home more than you want to be home. His love knows no bounds. Never compare your pallid, capricious, conditional human love with my Father's love. He is God not man.[56]

Another way that Kristi used Scripture to re-direct her thoughts onto God was to use the Jesus Prayer: "Lord Jesus Christ have mercy on me."[57] To this day when critical

---

[55] Brennan Manning, *Stranger to Self-Hatred* (Dimension Books: 1982), p. 33-34.

[56] Brennan Manning, *Stranger to Self-Hatred* (Dimension Books: 1982), p. 40, 42.

[57] In the third century the Desert Fathers used the Jesus Prayer to help them "pray without ceasing" (1 Thessalonians 5:17). They got this from the Psalmist's recurring cry, "Lord, have mercy on me" and from the tax collector and others in the New Testament who cried out to Christ for mercy.

thoughts ambush her and throw her down into feeling bad about herself Kristi says, "I take my feelings of failure and inadequacy and I confess those to the Lord. Then I pray the Jesus Prayer slowly over and over till I sense that I've received his mercy. This focuses me on the cross and Christ being enough for me – it stops my self-criticism. It becomes okay that I'm not enough because Christ is and he gives himself to me – he is what I really need!"

Kristi also has learned to stay out of self-hatred by *incarnating* for others God's word of mercy to her. When feelings of shame start to come upon her she focuses on something good that she can do for somebody else. She explains, "It helps to distract me from my feelings of worthlessness if I serve somebody in a position of obvious need. In this way I get my eyes off of myself and am able to participate with God in serving somebody else out of love for him. This is not about denying my needs or earning God's favor – it's about getting in the flow of God's grace."

"If none of these ways work," Kristi says, "and I'm really stuck in feelings of shame then I turn on worship music and start praising God. That always helps."

The Way of the Pilgrim and the Pilgrim Continues his Way (Episcopal Book Club: 1952, originally published in 1858 by an anonymous author) tells the charming and inspiring story of how the Jesus Prayer brought healing and transformation to an anonymous Russian pilgrim and the many people he touched. See my article on SoulShepherding.org, "The Jesus Prayer: A Little Prayer and a Big Change."

Spiritual Exercise: Memorize Scripture

As you go about your day what do you think about? Every moment of every day you and I have the freedom to think about *whatever we want*. The thoughts that you choose to dwell on are the most important factor not only in how you feel, but also what you say and do and ultimately the person you become. "We live at the mercy of our ideas," Dallas Willard summarizes.

The way to overcome anxious thought patterns like self-criticism (or any negative attachment for that matter) is with a positive connection to God. Memorizing Scripture and then using it for meditation and prayer is an indispensible way to engage our minds, and ultimate our whole person, with God. I know of no better way to re-direct worries than to put my thoughts on God's Word and then let the Holy Spirit use the Scripture to teach me and draw me into greater intimacy with God. With the Word of God revealed to me as the risen Christ I have the Counselor and *Friend* that I need. I can then let go of the Worry Witch and embrace the Prince of Peace.

When you memorize Scripture you're taking its structure, wisdom, and grace inside your mind. Once God's words and the deep, life-giving insights it brings are in your thoughts then they can get into your heart to form your will and permeate your body, social interactions, and soul. The Proverb is true: "As a person thinks in his heart that's who he or she becomes" (Proverbs 23:7, paraphrase). And when you hide Scripture in your heart (Psalm 119:11) then you can take it with you wherever you go so that at any time – while driving, waiting in line, brushing your teeth, or laying in bed unable to sleep – you can mull over God's Word and let it lead you in prayer.

Memorize *Loooong* Passages

The typical approach to Scripture memory, popularized by the evangelical organizations like the Navigators and utilized recently by Rick Warren in *The Purpose Driven Life*, is to memorize lots of individual verses or short passages on topical themes. This is a helpful approach for learning key doctrinal points, witnessing for Christ, and also for simple meditations like Breath Prayers. However, the Bible was not given in verse format, but in *flowing conversations.*

Memorizing larger sections of Scripture in paragraphs or whole chapters dramatically *deepens* our experience with God's Word. Memorizing passages from the Bible is powerful for our spiritual formation in Christ because it helps us to drink from the flow of Living Waters that's in the Bible. As we memorize a section of Scripture it's *life-giving properties*[58] naturally lead us to meditate and pray – we can simply let the Holy Spirit carry us along, renewing our minds in the goodness and wisdom of God that's revealed in his words.

Martin Luther taught that to pray over a paragraph or a chapter from the Bible that you've memorized is like carrying around a *pocket lighter* that can warm you up to God's presence at any time. In his pastoral letter to his barber he wrote:

---

[58] So the writer to Hebrews says that, "The word of God is living and active" (Hebrews 4:12). In other words, Scripture it is not only true, it is *real* – it is *living*. When God speaks he creates life!

A good prayer should not be lengthy or drawn out, but frequent and ardent. It is enough to consider one section or half of a section [of God's word] which kindles a fire in the heart. This the Spirit will grant us and continually instruct us in when, by God's word, our hearts have been cleared and freed of outside thoughts and concerns...

With practice one can take the Ten Commandments on one day, a Psalm or chapter of Holy Scripture the next day and use them as a flint and a steel to kindle a flame in the heart.[59]

Another important aspect of memorizing long passages of Scripture, rather than only verses, is that it forces you to submit to God's Word. We tend to try to make the Bible say what we want it to say! But this is very hard to take Scripture out of context when you take it in through long passages.

The thought of memorizing a whole chapter of Scripture might be intimidating to you. Just don't start with Psalm 119 – the longest chapter in the Bible! Instead start with Psalm 23 or one of the other "electric passages" from Scripture.[60] Memory is like a muscle so if you start small and exercise your mind over time then you'll be surprised by how much Scripture you'll be able to memorize!

---

[59] Martin Luther, *A Simple Way to Pray* (Westminster John Knox Press: 2000), p. 56 (originally published in 1535).

[60] All Scripture is inspired by God and authoritative to guide our lives, but some of it is *electric!* For a list of my favorite paragraphs and chapters of the Bible to memorize see my article, "Electric Passages of the Bible to Memorize" on SoulShepherding.org.

Mostly, Scripture memory requires repetition. Repeating words over and over can brand them into your brain, especially as you concentrate and seek to understand what you're reading. Seeing insights and connections in the passage will help you to remember. Also, your memory will be greatly aided if you associate visual images with the Scripture. To remember lists it's helpful to use acronyms.

Be Renewed in Romans 8
"Be transformed by the renewing of your mind," Paul taught us (Romans 12:1). God's Word diagnoses (Hebrews 4:12), washes (Ephesians 5:26), and gives life (Genesis 1, Matthew 4:4) to our minds and ultimately our whole being when we study it, meditate on it, memorize it, and pray through it with an open heart, applying it specifically to our needs and struggles.

A powerful chapter to memorize and one that is particularly helpful if you struggle with feeling bad about yourself is Romans 8. This is an amazing chapter of the Bible! It begins and ends by reinforcing the blessings of being "in Christ" and all throughout it is full of God's gracious promises. Here God teaches us how to *tap into the electric current of God's Spirit and resurrection life.* Eighteen times the Holy Spirit is named in this one chapter, where as he is only named ten times in the other fifteen chapters of Romans combined.

The eighth chapter of Romans was key for helping Kristi to fill her heart with God's grace. She was meeting with Jane Willard (Dallas' wife) for some healing prayer sessions and Jane suggested that Kristi memorize Romans 8. Kristi recalls, "I read it and re-read it. I read it in every version I could find. I read commentaries and asked people about what it meant, but it seemed so hard to understand and so impersonal. For me it was dry, wordy, confusing."

But Kristi printed out Romans 8 on a sheet of paper anyway. She carried it with her for a whole year, memorizing it little-by-little." She reports, "As I memorized it then it came to life for me and became very personal, healing, and beautiful. I began to experience the truths of Romans 8 that overcome my feelings of self-hatred: I'm not under condemnation. The Father has chosen me and justified me. I've been given the spirit of adoption and the Holy Spirit testifies that I'm God's child and helps me with my weakness. Jesus is the only one who has the right to judge me and he is interceding for me. So nobody can bring any charge against me! Nobody or no thing can separate me from God's love!"

Kristi says to people, "If I can memorize Romans 8 then you can too!" But you many not want to start there. There are two other ways that you can squeeze much of the juice out from Romans 8 without memorizing the whole chapter. You can memorize a condensed version that includes key verses.[61]

---

[61] Here's my version of Romans 8 Condensed:

Therefore, there is now no condemnation for those who are in Christ Jesus, because through Christ Jesus the law of the Spirit of life set me free from the law of sin and death... The mind set on [natural human abilities] is death, but the mind controlled by the Spirit is life and peace... If the Spirit of him who raised Jesus from the dead is living in you, he who raised Christ from the dead will also give life to your mortal bodies through his Spirit, who lives in you...

Those who are led by the Spirit of God are sons [and daughters] of God. For you did not receive a spirit that makes you a slave again to

Or you can meditate on the Romans 8 Promises for Disciples of Jesus, putting your name in each one:[62]

There is no condemnation for _____, who is in Christ Jesus (vs. 1)

The Spirit has set _____ free from sin and death (vs. 2)

The Spirit who raised Jesus from the dead lives in and is energizing _____ (vs. 11)

_____ is led by God and thus is a child of God (vs. 14)

_____ can call God "Abba" or Daddy! (vs. 15)

---

fear, but you received the Spirit of adoption. And by him we cry, "Abba, Father." The Spirit himself testifies with our spirit that we are God's children. Now if we are children, then we are heirs—heirs of God and co-heirs with Christ, if indeed we share in his sufferings in order that we may also share in his glory...

In the same way, the Spirit helps us in our weakness. We do not know what we ought to pray for, but the Spirit himself intercedes for us with groans that words cannot express...

And we know that in all things God works for the good of those who love him, who have been called according to his purpose. For those God foreknew he also predestined to be conformed to the likeness of his Son...

What, then, shall we say in response to this? If God is for us, who can be against us? He who did not spare his own Son, but gave him up for us all—how will he not also, along with him, graciously give us all things? Who will bring any charge against those whom God has chosen? It is God who justifies. Who is he that condemns? Christ Jesus, who died—more than that, who was raised to life—is at the right hand of God and is also interceding for us...

We are more than conquerors through him who loved us...

[Nothing] will be able to separate us from the love of God that is in Christ Jesus our Lord. (Romans 8:1-2, 6, 11, 14-17, 26, 28-29, 31-34, 37, 39)

[62] Remember that the promises of the Bible are not just there for the grabbing! They are designed to work in the lives of people who are apprenticing themselves to the Lord Jesus Christ!

Through Christ _____ is an heir of God, inheriting divine blessings (vs. 17)

_____'s body will be redeemed, set free and made whole (vs. 23)

The Spirit helps _____'s weaknesses with intercessions from deep inside (vs. 26)

All things work together for the good of _____ who loves God and is called according to his purpose (vs. 28)

God takes initiative to know, guide, call, justify, and glorify _____, helping _____ to become more and more like Jesus (vs. 29-30)

If God is for _____ then who can be against _____? (vs. 31)

In all things _____ is more than a conqueror through Christ's love (vs. 37)

Nothing – absolutely nothing! – can separate _____ from the love God that is in Christ (vs. 38-39).

Breath Prayer
Pick one of the Romans 8 Promises for Disciples of Jesus to use as a Breath Prayer this week. Ask God to lead you to the verse that you need most. You may want to paraphrase the wording to have a short, flowing prayer to use for times of quiet saturation and also to carry with you for meditation as you go about your day.

For instance, try this helpful, Spirit-lifting Breath Prayer based on verse 1: "In Christ... there is no condemnation for me."

Slowly breathe in the wonderful words of your blessed position before God: "In Christ..." Hold your breath and your Lord sweetly in your heart... Exhale and release any feelings of guilt or badness: "There is no condemnation for me."

God may draw you to use one these other Romans 8 Breath Prayer options (following the same breathe in... breathe out pattern), or he might inspire you to from our own little prayer:
"Holy Spirit... set me free!" (from verse 2)
"Spirit of Christ raise me up with you... forever" (from verse 11)
"Abba... I belong to you" (from verse 15)
"God is for me... who can be against me" (from verse 31)
"In the love of Christ... I am a conqueror" (from verse 37)

Salty Questions

One of the primary ways that we experience God's love is when we, as disciples of Jesus, share our hearts and listen to one another. These questions are meant to help you and your friend or group to "pass the salt" around the table of fellowship. Salt preserves (sometimes we don't know what we've learned until we verbalize it), adds flavor (conversations that draw us closer to Christ are the sweetest of all), and makes us thirsty (when we experience God we always desire more of him).

What are you learning about how living in Jesus' easy yoke of mercy sets you free from self-condemnation?

Do you criticize or condemn yourself? What is an example?

This week how has putting your thoughts on Scripture helped you to connect with God's grace and mercy through Christ?

You Can Live in Jesus' Easy Yoke: Lesson #5
Hurry Up and Be Still

I was running late to a seminar and so I was in a hurry. The lady in the car in front of me started slowing to a stop right in front of me as she meandered into the left turn lane. "Why is it always when I'm rushing that I get behind a slow driver?"

Then to make matters worse, the light started to turn red. I pushed through.

Then I got to my left turn and the sign said: "No left turns from 6:30 am to 9:00 am." It was 8:35 am. I turned left anyway. *I'm almost there. Five minutes late and counting.*

Approaching the parking lot there was a stop sign. Nobody was around so I looked both ways, rolled through it and parked.

As I got out of my car it hit me: *I just broke three traffic laws and I'm going to a "Lead Like Jesus Seminar!" Well, at least I don't have a fish on my car!* As you can imagine, I slunk my way into the building hoping that no one would recognize me!

Then, as if that wasn't enough conviction, at the seminar Ken Blanchard stressed the importance for Christian leaders of slowing down their pace and putting margin in their schedules. I knew that God was talking to me! To influence people for God like Jesus did I needed to make more *space* in my life by allowing more time for what is most important.

That was seven years ago. It was less than a year after a spiritual renewal in which God had gotten a hold of my heart anew. I rededicated myself to – in the words that Ray Ortlund encouraged me with – "Be all and only for Jesus."[63]

Back then I often relied on adrenaline to keep up a fast pace. And when I slowed down and did not do anything "productive" for an extended period of time, like on a long weekend in Palm Springs, I felt restless, bored, empty, and depressed (this is adrenaline withdrawal).

But everything changed for me when I heard God whisper to my heart: "Be still and know that I am God" (Psalm 46:10). Little-by-little, the Lord drew me into a slower, quieter, and less driven life – he wooed me into the delights of a more intimate relationship with himself! But before I tell you how you can grow in God's peace with me let's consider the effect that being in a hurry has on our life with God and one another.

Always Late
Kent was ten minutes late for his meeting with me again. He tried to make a joke of it, "I'm sorry. I guess I need 25 hours in my day!" Invariably he ran late for meetings and events because he was always trying to squeeze one more thing into his day.

Kent complained about having too much to do and being tired of rushing around all the time. He thought that his hurried, overcrowded life was inevitable for him as a

---

[63] Ray Ortlund, *Lord Make My Life a Miracle* (Regal Books:1974).

pastor who had a family and lived in Orange County, CA in the 21st Century. But being an adrenaline addict in recovery myself, I knew better! So I spoke the truth in love to him, "I think you like being in a hurry and doing so much. Maybe the feeling of urgency and importance energizes you. And besides it drives you finger-drumming, foot-tapping crazy when you have to wait for people!"

Kent disagreed with me. I just smiled and left the matter in God's hands.

Sure enough, the night before Kent's next appointment with me he had a dream that he took his wife and two girls on a picnic. As they walked along he was carrying the picnic lunch and the lawn chairs and his wife was holding the hands of their little girls. And he led his family to sit down together *on the fast lane of the freeway!*

So there they were trying to enjoy their picnic lunch while cars kept racing by! Car after car that was driving in the fast lane had to slow down and move over a lane in order not to hit them. But then a truck came barreling down the freeway, close behind a car, and not seeing them sitting there, it was about to run into his wife!

It was then that Kent woke up – in his nightmare and in his life! He told me about his frightening dream and said, "You were right in what you said to me last week. I am going too fast. My wife has been trying to tell me the same thing."

Kent's conversations with me and the readings I gave him helped him to become more aware of how much he was using adrenaline to stay keyed up. He began to realize that he was choosing to fill up his calendar and to race from thing to thing. And that this hurried lifestyle was keeping him from enjoying God's peace, hearing his voice, and being more attentive to people in his life. To be sure, from time to time Kent had sought to be nourished by the God of Peace, like on extended family vacations or spiritual retreats. But it would always take him a long time to enter into a relaxed state of being and once he returned to his daily responsibilities he would go right back to his hurried self.

Depending on Adrenaline
Kent was depending on adrenaline. He had what some medical doctors call "hurry sickness." An important part of helping Kent learn to slow down was to show him the underlying attitudes that perpetuated his hurried and harried approach to life. People like Kent live by damaging, false narratives for life like:
"If you don't hurry you're going to miss out"
"Faster is better"
"Multi-tasking is essential to success"
"More excitement is always good"
"I shouldn't have to wait on anyone (I have too much to do. I'm too important)"

Dr. Archibald Hart believes that "adrenaline dependence" has become the greatest addiction problem in America today. People actually become "hooked" on the energy, pleasure, and confidence that come when the body's stress hormones – primarily adrenaline and cortisol – are released in emergencies.[64]

---

[64] Archibald Hart, *The Hidden Link Between Adrenaline and Stress.*

God has designed our bodies wonderfully and it is a great gift that we have this instinctive, adrenal "fight or flight" response to danger that infuses us with vitality and well-being. Adrenaline alerts us to grab our child's hand at the curb when a car races by. It gives us confidence when we are giving a very important presentation. It energizes us when we need to overcome a challenge or work through a stressful conflict. It cushions us when we get bad news. We need adrenaline to handle real life emergencies like these.

But it's a problem for us when we misuse adrenaline to live "keyed up," in a hurry, flitting about in anxious activity, or treating daily stresses as urgent situations.

Hurry Sickness Survey

As was true for Kent and myself, you may be relying on adrenaline in unhealthy ways and not even know it! Try my self-test to see if you might be in danger of having hurry sickness. Answer each question below with "yes" (mostly true for you) or "no" (mostly *not* true for you). Then circle each "yes" answer...

- Are you often in a hurry, rushing from one thing to the next?
- During a typical day do you work with intensity on something that seems urgent?
- Do you tend to do two or three things at once to be more efficient?
- Are you productive, busy, or active almost all the time?
- Do you regularly rely on caffeine to feel energetic and focused?

- If you're not working on something do you rely on stimulation from activity, entertainment, or noise?
- When you're resting do you feel fidgety, pace, drum your fingers, tap your feet, or chew fast?
- If you're idle do you feel guilty or restless?
- When you're waiting are you usually uncomfortably impatient (e.g., looking at your watch, getting upset, or counting items in the short order line)?
- When you go to bed at night do you typically think about all the things that you didn't get done and need to get done?
- When you go on vacation do you feel empty, bored, or depressed?
- Do you often have physical stress symptoms like gastric distress, rapid heartbeat, headaches, muscle pain, teeth grinding at night, and sleep problems?

If you have four or more yes answers you may have hurry sickness. You might be depending on adrenaline (and related hormones like cortisol) to manage your daily stresses. Living in a rush and under pressure puts our bodies at risk of stress-related illness. It also hinders our relationships – people don't feel loved if we don't take the time to notice them, listen to them, and *just be with them.* And we can't hear God's voice very well if we're living in the fast lane.[65]

---

[65] Learning to hear and trust God's voice is essential to our spiritual growth and to effective living. Slowing down is one of the most important things we can do to begin to tune into the Holy Spirit's guidance. If you're weaving in and out of traffic it's hard to read your GPS map! I use GPS to teach listening to God through the "the three lights" (1) God's Word, (2) Providence or life circumstances, (3) Spirit-

Why Depend on Adrenaline?

Why do people depend on adrenaline? Why live in the fast lane instead of Jesus' easy yoke? Because we want to rely on ourselves to make our lives work better – we want to be in control. Pastors may use adrenaline to get up for their sermon. Business people may rely on it to get through their 60-hour workweek. Parents may depend on it to deal with their children and get them from one activity to the next. Students who go to classes and work all day and then study late into the night use it to stay alert while depriving themselves of sleep. It seems like we have so much to do and our society is changing so fast – *we feel we must get keyed up to keep up!*

Besides, everyone else is doing it, aren't they? Doesn't everyone these days rely on extra coffee or other caffeinated drinks to stay in top form? Isn't it normal to live in a hurry going from one pressure to the next? Doesn't the Bible teach us to do more in less time when it says, "Redeem the time for the days are evil"? (Ephesians 5:16, KJV) Indeed, it seems that way. So fast-paced living is not only socially acceptable, it's admired and rewarded in our society, perhaps especially so in our Christian culture today.[66]

---

impressions that God sends to our minds and hearts. Dallas Willard's book on guidance, *Hearing God: Developing a Conversational Relationship with God* (InterVarsity Press: 1999) is very helpful. He originally published it as *In Search of Guidance* in 1984.

[66] We might think that it was easier to be patient in the simpler societies of times past. No doubt, it is true that the innumerable technological "time saving devices" that we have today, from microwaves to iphones, just keep complicating our lives and tempting us to multi-task and hurry so that we can get more done in less time!

But I think the most important reason why we may rely on adrenaline is simply because *it feels good!* We all want to feel alive, energized, and important – and recruiting our body's speed chemicals is a way to make ourselves feel that way, rather than depending on God and waiting for his provision.

Like people struggling with other types of compulsive behaviors, adrenaline abusers often have an underlying depression. Without adrenaline flowing they may feel empty inside – or insignificant. So they rush around doing "urgent" things, to help them feel alive and important. They keep getting keyed up to feel confident and energized. They take on pressures and they hurry to get more accomplished. Or they find something new, challenging, or exciting to get themselves stimulated.

(Have you ever found yourself impatient while you're waiting for your food to come out of the microwave?!) And it is true that establishing the rhythms of your life around sunrise and sunset – rather than your own ability to flip a switch, which was not possible until relatively recent generations – helps us to slow down. And we all have experienced how being connected to nature, which was natural for people in an agricultural society, helps us to be more relaxed and soulful.

But ever since we left the Garden of Eden we have had to deal our own and other people's sinful nature and the wiles of Satan and his demons, along with weeds and all sorts of irritations that come with being in a fallen world. Stress has always been a part of human life and it is our *attitude* about daily pressures that causes impatience. That's true today and it was true thousands of years ago.

Love is...
If you were asked, "What is love?" How would you answer? Many people think love is a desire or a feeling and that's why we say, "I *love* chocolate cake!" But really we just want to eat it! Sadly, this is the attitude that many take into other relationships, especially marriage. And this is why we "fall" in and out of love so easily.

Other people know better and define love by expressions of care or generosity, which are essential to love. But very few of us would define love as the Apostle Paul did, beginning by saying: "Love is patient..." (1 Corinthians 13:4). Why does Paul focus on patience? Why does he indicate that love begins with being long-suffering? For many of us, patience is very difficult! You know the joke, "Never pray for patience!"

Love is patient. Let's try putting that in some other wording to help us understand what Paul is saying and why he begins his description of love with being patient: "Love endures and suffers long; it is not easily irritated or impulsive. Love moves *sloooow* – it is *never in a hurry* and it is always willing to wait. Love makes time to notice other people. It takes time to thank God for the wonders of his creation all around us."

Taking time – *not being in a hurry* – is the beginning of Love. Paul begins defining love by focusing on patience because all the other attributes of love depend on patience. If we're in a hurry our ability to love is compromised. Any expression of love that you can think of – listening, doing a kindness, offering a compliment, giving a gift, or praying for someone – requires time. Setting aside time is what enables us to pay attention to others and what they need and then to respond to them with kindness. Moving at a *relaxed pace* – not trying to do too much, too fast – gives our soul the space it needs to breathe in God's Spirit. And as we connect with the God *who is love* then we receive his blessing and power to be compassionate, kind, and generous toward others.

The point is that in 1 Corinthians 13 Paul is speaking of Love. Notice I said, *Love* not love. Don't read the Bible's Love Chapter by putting your name in it, "Bill is patient. Bill is kind..." I can't live up to that and neither can you! That mentality generates pressure to measure up or guilt about falling short. And even if you seem to succeed you'll be relying on your flesh (your natural human abilities), not on God, and thus you'll be feeding pride. It's not you or I that is patient or kind – it is Love.

So we need to first read 1 Corinthians 13 by putting the name of the Lord in there: *"God* is patient with me. *God* is kind to me..."* As God's love lives in us through Christ then we will naturally be able to share it with others. Yes, "God is love... We love because he first loved us" (1 John 4:16, 19). That's Jesus' Good News Gospel! We can grow in the grace of God. We can count on the kindness of the King. This is a much better narrative for our lives than, "Hurry up or you'll miss out!"

Jesus' Quiet, Hidden Years
Jesus learned that love is patient early in his life. The Gospels are silent about the first eighteen years of Jesus' adult life, from ages 12 to 30, but we can surmise from what the Gospels do say that he worked an ordinary carpenter or stonecutter in the country village of Nazareth. Today we might call him a "blue collar worker."

I can imagine Jesus working as a common laborer taking his time to do a good job for his customers, working the wood with his hands and smoothing it out. I can picture him serving complaining customers with a smile, sweating for the rich who hired him to do a job, blessing the aristocrats when they treated him like low life, rejoicing in menial work because his Abba was at his side, loaning out his tools to people who didn't return them, and working long hours to bring home food and goods for his widowed mother and younger siblings.

The Son of God who was to be the Savior of world seemingly "wasted" most of his adult life in his incarnation laboring with his hands in obscurity. Apparently, he didn't give any notable sermons or perform any healings or make any disciples. Nobody even knew who he was except Mary had a few ideas about it. This was the Father's plan and Jesus followed it.

Then I think about Jesus and his example in these hidden years – and my heart melts with appreciation for the humble, beautiful way of the incarnation of God in Christ. Jesus had far and away the most demanding call upon his life that any human being will ever have and yet he wasn't in a rush to get going and he never worried or pushed to make things happen. He was content for decades to learn and grow quietly, practicing his faith in simple village life and ordinary work. He found meaning and joy in loving God and his neighbors (meaning, literally, "whatever boor is nearby at the moment!") in the midst of daily life.

Jesus was Interruptible

The *unhurried way* that Jesus practiced in his hidden years he lived out in the three years of his public ministry. He waited with the Father in prayer early in the morning before he ministered to people. He waited to select his disciples. He waited for the right time to go to his last Passover feast. He waited to go to Lazarus who was dying. He walked from place to place at the leisurely pace of conversation and prayer. He was always relaxed in the easy yoke of the Father.

Because Jesus lived unhurried and relaxed he was interruptible. Have you ever noticed this? To Jesus needy people were never an "interruption"! They pulled his robe in the crowd, *yelled* at him from the other side of the street, set children at his feet when he was trying to preach a message, followed him when he went away for solitude and prayer, peppered him with questions, called out at him from trees, cut a hole in the roof and dropped at his feet...

People continually came at Jesus from all directions! They were *desperate* for the life he offered! In fact, if you removed all the so-called "interruptions" from Jesus' ministry then there wouldn't be much ministry left! Most of the encounters he had with people were unscheduled and occurred as he was on his way from one thing to another.

This makes me think... *Could it be that God ordains our steps – and our stops?*[67] Maybe I should welcome the yellow light that is about to turn red and not rush through, but stop. *Stop!* Don't be in such a hurry. Pause. Take a breath. Notice people around me. Pray.

Jesus' "Little Way"

Jesus' unhurried pace of life, living in the easy yoke of the Father, is what enabled him to love. Perhaps the true greatness of Jesus is best seen in the many little, ordinary ways that he loved the people near him...

Jesus repaired broken chairs. He fixed breakfast. He washed feet. He touched lepers. He healed sick people. He played with children. He listened to the broken-hearted. He went to parties with social outcasts. He invited the poor into the Kingdom of the Heavens. Day after day for three years he quietly taught a few uneducated men and women how to be his apprentices in kingdom living.[68] He loved his enemies, blessed those who cursed him, and prayed for those who persecuted him.

And as you know, Jesus, taught us to follow his way of being a loving servant to others:

---

[67] George Mueller (1805-1898), an English evangelist and philanthropist who established many orphanages, said, "The stops of a good man, as well as his steps, are ordered by the Lord."

[68] There were 120 disciples that followed Jesus' instructions (given just before he ascended and disappeared in the heavens) to wait for the coming Holy Spirit (Acts 1:15). These are the ones God used to birth the Church.

Do your good deeds in secret... Whoever wants to be great must become the servant... The first shall be last and the last shall be first... Blessed are the merciful... Give and it shall be given unto you... It's more blessed to give than to receive... Give a cup of cold water... Feed the hungry, care for the sick, visit those in prison... Wash one another's feet... Welcome little children... Love your enemies... Bless those who insult you... Pray for those who persecute you... Give away your coat... Go the extra mile... As you do unto the least of these so you've done unto me.[69]

Richard Foster explained how Thérèse of Lisieux[70] (1873-1897) in her short life followed Jesus' example of humble service for other people:

This Little Way, as she called it, is deceptively simple. It is in short, to seek out the menial job, to welcome unjust criticism, to befriend those who annoy us, to help those who are ungrateful. For her part, Therese was convinced

---

[69] Paraphrases from Matthew 6:4, Matthew 20:26, Mark 9:35, Luke 6:38, Acts 20:35, Matthew 10:42, Luke 10:37, Matthew 25:34-36, John 13:14, Matthew 18:5, Matthew 22:39, Luke 6:27-28, Matthew 5:40-41, Matthew 25:40.

[70] Thérèse of Lisieux felt called by God at the age of 14 to dedicate her life to Jesus. She became a nun one year later, joining her two older sisters in the enclosed Carmelite community of Lisieux, Normandy. After nine years of dedicated service she became ill and died of tuberculosis in 1897 at the age of 24. Because of her sweet, humble love for God and neighbor she became known as "The Little Flower of Jesus" and one of the greatest saints of her era.

that these "trifles" pleased Jesus more than the great deeds of recognized holiness.

The beauty of the Little Way is how utterly available it is to everyone. From the child to the adult, from the sophisticated to the simple, from the most powerful to the least influential, all can undertake this ministry of small things. The opportunities to live in this way come to us constantly, while the great fidelities happen only now and again. Almost daily we can give smiling service to nagging co-workers, listen attentively to silly bores, express little kindnesses without making a fuss.[71]

Serving God in the Little Way doesn't get much attention. Most people would rather do great things for God and be applauded by large crowds. But it's the quiet, humble way of simply giving a cup of cold water in Jesus' name that gives these little kindnesses their great value. They lend dignity and hope to those who need it desperately. They also work to conquer our own selfish ambition and pride, freeing us up even further to slow down, notice others and bless them.

Like Thérèse of Lisieux, we can learn to follow Jesus into this Little Way – *but only if we first imitate the way he slowed down to appreciate the Father and abide in his love in the moment.* If Jesus had lived at a face pace, continually under pressure to do more, relying on himself and not the Father with him, then he would not have been able to be such a loving servant to the people near him.

---

[71] *Prayer* by Richard Foster, 1990, page 62.

Unhurried with Jesus

In Jerusalem I visited the site where the temple used to be and I walked the same south entry steps that Jesus walked on. I noticed that the steps were irregular – they varied in length, some being long and others being short. I learned that this was done to *slow people down as they came to worship!* By walking more slowly they would be helped to pray and be more attentive to God and receptive to his word.[72] Imagine if we did that in our churches today! Sadly, most of us rush into church distracted and get there five minutes late.

In Jesus' day there was a saying, "A noble person is known by... the way he walks."[73] Distinguished men did not run – they walked and the more honorable they were *the slower they walked.* The Bible has a lot to say about "the way of the upright." It's referred to 97 times in the Psalms alone. To walk uprightly is to walk with God, looking to him in the heavens all around you as you walk. This is not done helter skelter! It's done with care and deliberateness; it's done patiently. When Jesus said, "I am the way to the Father" (John 14:6, paraphrase) he was inviting us into his unhurried rhythms of grace (Matthew 11:28-30, MSG).

Recently I was reading a book in which a respected Christian teacher said that Jesus did not have much to say about living without hurry. It's true that the Gospels don't

---

[72] Gary M. Burge, *Jesus, the Middle Eastern Storyteller* (Zondervan, 2009), p. 26.

[73] Sirach 19:29-30. From the Jewish apocrypha (considered a Deuterocanonical book by Protestants) written in the second century BC.

record lots of instances of Jesus saying the words: "Do not hurry!" But there are many other ways of saying the same thing!

Jesus' whole life example is one of being unhurried. And this was also an important theme in his teachings:

Don't be in such a hurry... Listen... Whoever has ears to hear, listen... Don't worry... Who of you by worrying can add a single hour to his life?... Peace... Come to me... Take my yoke upon you and you will find rest for your souls for my yoke is easy and my burden is light... Walk with me in my unforced rhythms of grace... Don't run in the dark! Walk with me in the light so you don't stumble... Peace! Be still... Come away with me by yourselves to a quiet place and rest... Stop your busy work to sit at my feet and listen to my words... Watch and pray... Be constantly alert... Always pray... Wait for the gift of the Holy Spirit that my Father promised... Take time to love your neighbor.[74]

Jesus' example was that he was never in a hurry – *except to go the cross and die for us!* When the Father said it was time he turned and headed straight for Jerusalem, leading his disciples with resolve (Mark 10:32 and Luke 19:28, MSG). Jesus' only hurry throughout his life was to listen to his Father and to obey him.

---

[74] Paraphrases from Matthew 16:27 (MSG), Matthew 15:10, Matthew 11:15, Matthew 6:25-27, Luke 24:36, Matthew 11:28-30 (NIV and MSG), John 12:35, Mark 4:39 (NKJV), Mark 6:31 (NASB), Luke 10:38-42, Matthew 26:41, Mark 13:33 (AMP), Luke 18:1, Acts 1:4, Luke 10:36-37.

We are wise to "Hurry Up and Be Still" with Jesus, to listen to and obey the Father with him. As we learn to slow down and walk in Jesus' easy yoke it helps us to hear God's voice and to love others as God loves us.

Be Still as the Lake at Dawn
I thank God that by his grace he can help hurried people like me to be still in God's presence. Of course, sometimes I slip back into my old rut and need to remind myself to slow down to listen to the Lord and follow his leading! Because I have learned not to hurry I can tell you with confidence, as I told Kent, that slowing down to pay attention and respond to God in all things is a much better narrative for life than thinking that daily stresses are urgencies and I must hurry up so I don't miss out an opportunity to accomplish something.

For instance, one morning a couple of years ago I was enjoying a Sabbath day for prayer and I was reciting Psalm 46 and praying through it. I was particularly drawn to the words God spoke to the Psalmist: "Be still and know that I am God" (Psalm 46:10).

I was meditating on this verse by using different translations and paraphrases in order to bring out deeper meaning for me, like a bee sucking more and more nectar out of a flower...
"Quiet your heart, rely on me – the Spirit of Christ, the I AM – living and breathing in you" (my paraphrase).
"Step out of the traffic! Take a long, loving look at me, your High God" (MSG).
"Our God says, 'Calm down, and learn that I am God'" (CEV).

"Cease striving and know that I am God" (Dallas Willard's paraphrase).

We like to sing these beloved "Be still" words of Psalm 46 as if they were a lullaby. We like to quote them or print them with serene pictures as if they belonged in a peaceful monastery setting. There is nothing wrong with these things, but we need to be careful lest we strip the Word of God of its power – these are far more than pretty words!

The context of Psalm 46 is the conflict and chaos that comes with storms, earthquakes, tidal waves, collapsing governments, and nations at war. God is teaching the Psalmist to look beyond the visible, stressful circumstances and to see into the invisible Kingdom of the heavens in our midst where, "There is a river whose streams make glad the city of God" (verse 4) and "The Lord Almighty is with us; the God of Jacob is our fortress" (verses 7 and 11). The Lord alone is the one who "makes wars cease to the ends of the earth" (verse 9).

As I was meditating on Psalm 46 on that morning I was walking slowly around the lake near our home. The lake was like a sea of glass, reflecting sky and trees and birds. I could even see the fish swimming below. And yet, all was not peaceful, because I could hear the sounds of cars racing back and forth.[75]

---

[75] I have learned that it is very helpful when you can meditate on a Psalm or other Scripture in a nature setting like the one described in the passage. See my article, "Praying a Psalm in its Nature Setting" on SoulShepherding.org.

The noisy traffic beckoned me to hurry and get to work, reminding me that I had a lot to do! At the same time the quiet lake and the Word of God called out to me: "Be still and know that I am God." The visible world and the invisible kingdom of God were both calling to me – I chose to walk by faith and not by sight (2 Corinthians 4:18, 5:7).

In recent years the image of a still lake has become more and more deeply imbedded in my consciousness and my prayers. It draws me slow down. It invites me to be quiet. It opens my heart to listen. It centers me in God's presence. It reflects the kingdom of the heavens to me in surprising ways, as my prayer poem "Be Still" describes:

Be Still

Be still as the lake at Dawn
In a world that wakes to alarms and agendas:
Quietly rest so you can listen;
Breathe and open to your soul;
Wait patiently to receive what is to come,
Softly absorb the light as a looking glass.

Be still to know the I AM;
Let the "rush hour" pass by your silence:
The Voice whispers to create Life;
It swims and plays deep within you;
As holy feet step upon your waters
Heaven's Face smiles upon you
– and out from you.

Be still as the lake at Dawn;
Be still to know the I AM;
In a world that wakes to alarms and agendas
Let the "rush hour" pass by your silence.

Quietly rest so you can listen:
The Voice whispers to create Life;
Breathe and open to your soul
It swims and plays deep within you.

Wait patiently to receive what is to come,
As holy feet step upon your waters;
Softly absorb the light as a looking glass,
Heaven's Face smiles upon you
– and out from you.

The Best Time to Be Still

The best time to be still is the hardest for people with
hurry sickness: the first thing in the morning. C. S. Lewis
explains:

> The real problem of the Christ life comes where
> people do not usually look for it. It comes the very
> moment you wake up each morning. All your
> wishes and hopes for the day rush at you like wild
> animals. And the first job each morning consists
> simply in shoving them all back; in listening to that
> other voice, taking that other point of view, letting
> that other larger, stronger, quieter life come
> flowing in. And so on, all day. Standing back from
> all your natural fussings and frettings; coming in
> out of the wind.
>
> We can only do it for moments at first. But from
> those moments the new sort of life will be
> spreading through our system: because now we
> are letting Him work at the right part of us. It is the
> difference between paint, which is merely laid on

the surface, and a dye or stain which soaks right through.[76]

I am someone who wakes up hounded by the "wild animals!" Or if not hounded I am surely alert and ready to go when I awake. Some mornings I follow Lewis' admonition and I force myself to lay in bed and stay relaxed in the arms of Christ as I pray a Psalm and submit my day to the Lord. Dallas Willard does this. In the mornings he lays in bed to meditate and pray through the Lord's Prayer and Psalm 23. More commonly, I take the easier approach and pray (hopefully with a restful spirit!) as I'm doing my morning routine, sitting in a quiet spot with my Psalter open, or as I'm driving my car in solitude.

How Kent Learned to Be Still
How did Kent get out of the fast lane and into Jesus' easy yoke? What can we learn from Kent's story about being still in God's presence? He had to make a lifestyle change. He had to prostrate his productivity before the Lord. He had to remember to rely on the Holy Spirit instead of getting himself keyed up with moving fast and doing lots of things at once.

But Kent was not able just to stop relying on adrenaline. He had become dependent on it to feel energized and focused and confident. Hurrying from one urgency to the next and filling his day with anxious activity were unconscious habits. He liked being ultra productive. He liked coming in first place. He liked riding the wild animals!

---

[76] C. S. Lewis, *Mere Christianity* (Harper: originally published in 1952), p. 198.

I told Kent that he needed to "Hurry up and be still!" He needed to see that the one urgency for his life was learning to be still, connect with Christ, listen to him, and follow his lead. *This is urgent.* The prophet Isaiah sounded the alarm for the harried, distracted people of his day, but they didn't listen: "This is what the Sovereign LORD, the Holy One of Israel, says: 'In repentance and rest is your salvation, in quietness and trust is your strength, but you would have none of it'" (Isaiah 30:15).

Kent couldn't change his hurried habit immediately, but what he could do was learn to put margin in his schedule. Also he could start using the spaces he opened up in his day to pause, breathe, and meditate on Scripture. And doing these things did, over time and with practice, enable him to live at a slower pace and with greater peace. This is the power of using spiritual disciplines in our training to become more like Jesus. Recall that a spiritual discipline is something that we can directly do and with practice it changes us on the inside so that we become able, assisted by the grace of God, to do something that we could not do before.

Kent learned to slow down and appreciate God's presence in the transitions of his day. He made a prayer sanctuary of times that he was driving in his car or waiting in line. And in this way he grew in God's peace and in his ability to hear his voice. What a blessing this was for him, his family, and the church he pastored!

It isn't just hurried people like Kent that need to grow in God's peace through putting margin in their schedule. Anyone who tries to do too much, runs late for appointments, or struggles with impatience can benefit from learning to make good use of interludes in a day to be quiet and still in God's presence. It's they way to open our hearts to God and receive his Word.

Spiritual Exercise: Leave a Margin
Just as a page like this one has margins of white space around the edges, between paragraphs, and even a little bit between the lines and words so also our lives can have spaces. Margin is about saying no to a culture that rewards busyness and being overextended. It means saying no to your own desires for self-importance. It requires being able to say no to the inappropriate expectations other people; it frees us to live by the wisdom of the Bible: "Let the peace of Christ rule in your hearts" (Colossians 3:15).

The Benedictine monks use the Latin word "statio" to describe their practice of arriving early (making margin) before a prayer service, meeting, or other event. They find it important to have a few minutes to prepare their hearts in prayer for what's coming. Practicing statio helps them to listen to God.[77]

Of course, another important reason to plan to arrive early for meetings is to show consideration and respect for other people's time. It's disrespectful to make other people wait for you, as if your time is more important than theirs. (I'm not talking about being *perfectionistic* and never being late – that is a different problem that will discuss in a coming chapter!) Paul says, "In humility

---

[77] Joan Chittister, OSB, *Wisdom Distilled from the Daily: Living the Rule of St. Benedict Today* (Harper Collins: 1990).

consider others better than yourselves" (Philippians 2:3). Why? Not because you are unimportant! It is because God has humbled himself in Christ to serve you and to show you that you are very important. Our opportunity is to share the humble, sacrificial, eager-to-serve-love of Christ with others and one way we can do this is by being patient and prayerful when we wait for someone who is late.

Slowing down is difficult for hurried people! We have trouble accepting that *24-hours in a day is enough for us to do what God has called us to do that day* so we try to cram more in there!

In a busy, hectic season of life and ministry Pastor John Ortberg called his mentor Dallas Willard and asked him: "What do I need to do to be spiritually healthy?"

There was a long pause and then Dallas replied, "You must ruthlessly eliminate hurry from your life."

John then asked, "What else should I do?" (Perhaps he didn't like the first answer!)

After another long pause Dallas answered, "There is nothing else."[78]

Experiment with "Selah"
The word for margin in the Bible is *Selah*. 72 times the Psalmist prays or sings, "Selah" – often right in the middle

---

[78] John Ortberg tells this story in his article, "Taking Care of Busyness" in *Leadership Magazine,* Fall 1998 and in his book, *The Life you've Always Wanted: Spiritual Disciplines for Ordinary People,* p. 76. I've also heard him share this story extemporaneously in a sermon.

of a sentence! Selah probably means, "Pause to reflect in prayer." Selah is the disposition of the Psalmist when he prays: "But I have stilled and quieted my soul; like a weaned child with its mother, like a weaned child is my soul within me" (Psalm 131:2). Selah is an *unhurried space* to listen to God; it's a breather to help us appreciate God's loving presence. (It's occurred to me that perhaps Selah is the sound of breathing in, "Se" (say) and breathing out, "lah.") Try it now! – yes, right now, you could pause from reading and breathe a prayer: "Se... lah..." Breathing in deep, "Se..." And breathing out slowly, "lah..."

To learn to practice "Selah" *schedule less in your day* so that you can arrive early for meetings and use the extra few minutes to take a breather. At first this will probably be difficult for you if you are used to being in a hurry or trying to do too much. You may find yourself being late even though you try not to be. And when you do arrive early and have to wait you may be uncomfortable: perhaps your body feels restless, your mind keeps running through lists of things you need to do or problems you need to solve, and you feel irritated that someone is making you wait! (Just stop and think how often you've done that to people and thank God for his mercy. That will help you to share God's mercy with others.)

Learning something new is supposed to be difficult so don't worry about it – you're training! You're practicing making spaces in your schedule, taking prayer pauses, finding opportunities to breathe: "Se... lah..."

This week do an experiment. (Remember, it's only by putting into practice what God is teaching us that we grow in his grace.) Put some margin in your schedule as a way to

pay more attention to God in your midst and listen to him.
Try one or more of these ways of making space:
When you wake up stay in bed to meditate on a Scripture
and pray for five minutes or more
Leave early for an appointment and use the time to pray
for the meeting
Schedule some breaks in your day and use them to take a
breather in prayer
Move some things from today's "to do list" onto
tomorrow's list
Turn off the television or computer and sit quietly
Drive in the slow lane and meditate on Jesus' words, "The
first shall be last and the last shall be first."
Walk slowly to wherever you're going – feel the sun, see
the flowers, hear the birds, and say hello to people!
Take a Selah to pray Psalm 46:10 (see below)

Breath Prayer
For all of us – especially if we tend to hurry, don't like
waiting or feeling unproductive, or struggle with anxiety –
it is important to practice Scripture meditation at times
that are *not* stressful by making a generous space of "quiet
time" to practice statio or selah. Using Psalm 46:10 – "Be
still and know that I am God..." – as a Breath Prayer is a
great way to do this. If ever there was an "easy yoke"
training prayer this is it! It brings God's peace to you and
puts you into the position in which you can love others,
serving Christ in the Little Way.

Relaxed, deep breathing, as part of meditation on
Scripture, helps to slow down an antsy body and
jitterbugging thoughts. It's a way of relying on the Holy
Spirit within you to help your mind to focus on God and
your body to be still in his presence. You're heeding Jesus'

call to "watch and pray" with him; you're training with the Master and asking him to help you learn to become the kind of person who when stresses come on you that day you do not react with worry, agitation, impatience, or trying to control things, but remains in God's peace.

With practice using Breath Prayer meditations on Scripture you can grow to the point that when you find yourself waiting for a meeting or stuck in traffic you *naturally and easily* remain in Jesus' easy yoke, looking at the unanticipated slow down not as an irritation, but as an *opportunity* to take a breather and pray God's Word.

Let's practice a Breath Prayer with Psalm 46:10 now: Breathe in deep and slow as you think or whisper: "Be still and know that I am God..." (It takes a long, sloooow breath – you may need to practice this!) Then hold your breath and your concentration on God's Word of peace... Then breathe out... (Generally you want to give *about* seven to ten seconds for each prayer.)

You can pray God's Word into your body (which may be jittery!): "Be still and know that I am God..."

You can pray the Psalmist's prayer into any intrusive, anxious thoughts that come into your mind: "Be still and know that I am God..."

You can pray Scripture into any feelings of frustration at having to wait: "Be still and know that I am God..."

You can abide in Scripture to grow in your intimacy with the Lord, appreciating one of his names or an aspect of his character: "Be still and know that I am _____." (Fill in the blank with the name or characteristic of God that you especially need to connect with now, e.g., Provider, Healer, Counselor, Wonderful, Father, etc.)

What we want to do is to use this Breath Prayer to help us to "center down" in the way the old Quakers talked about.[79] We can make life, including our spiritual life, so complicated and cluttered! Getting off our hamster wheel, slowing down, doing less, and being still to listen and to know God are largely a matter of living a *simpler life.*

You might try my "Simplifying Breath Prayer" for a few minutes. (Simplicity[80] is the opposite of being ambitious and productive; it's to be your genuine self, fully present, before God and others as you do one thing well.)

Remember, it can help you to slow down and give your whole self to God if you take some slow, deep breaths as a bodily expression of prayer. And then you can gently take in the God's words to you in Psalm 46:10 by whispering or thinking the words as you breathe in slowly... Then holding your breath and your attention on God... Then exhaling slowly...

---

[79] Thomas Kelly (1893-1941) is one of the great Quaker writers who helps us to "center down" as we pray in Jesus' name. See *A Testament of Devotion,* written in 1941, page 46.

[80] *The Renovare Spiritual Formation Bible* defines simplicity or frugality as "The inward reality of single-hearted focus upon God and his kingdom, which results in an outward lifestyle of modesty, openness, and unpretentiousness and which disciplines our hunger for status, glamour, and luxury," p. 2313).

Be still and know that I am God...

Be still and know that I AM...

Be still and know...

Be still...

Be...

Salty Questions

Taking the time to share and pray from your heart with a friend or your small group is an important way to "Be still and know that [the Lord] is God." What is God saying to you? How are you experiencing him?

Maybe you're having some issues with stress or hurry. Maybe you're struggling to slow down and connect with God. Remember that accepting our trials as learning opportunities is crucial for our spiritual formation in Christ. So take courage and talk honestly with your spiritual friends and you'll be salty for God. This kind of soul talk is flavorful and it preserves learning. It draws people to Christ in you and makes them thirsty for more!

What is one thing that you're learning about Jesus' unhurried way of love?

Do you tend to be in a hurry? Rely on adrenaline to get keyed up? Get so busy that you don't enjoy the moment? Run late for meetings? What is an example?

What impact did it have on you to practice margin or take a selah in order to be still and pray Psalm 46:10?

You Can Live in Jesus' Easy Yoke: Lesson #6
Don't Overwork – Listen to the Birds

"How are you?" Steve asked me on the phone.

"Busy," I replied.

"What else is new?" he laughed. "Ever since we roomed together in college I've admired how disciplined and productive you are."

That was ten years ago. Although it was opposite of my friend's intention, I realized then that I was *too busy.* I was driven to be ultra "productive," always trying to do more in less time. To get more done I stayed up late *and* woke up early. I shaved with my electric razor while I drove to work. I routinely scheduled appointments back to back to back. I worked through lunch. I worked on Sundays. I worked in the office, at church, at home, and in my yard. I carried a heavy sense of responsibility everywhere I went. I didn't relax much. I didn't smile enough.

If you had gotten inside my head about fifteen years ago you might have heard anxious chatter that sounded like this:

I have to finish preparing for the class I'm teaching on depression tomorrow. I don't want to just "wing it" and do a bad job like last time, but when am I going to find time do that? I have a full day of therapy clients. On my lunch break I need to go through my list of messages and call people back – I don't feel like it, but I better because these people need help and besides I'm short on clients and we're under budget this month. Oh, and tonight we're going to Kristi's parents' house to celebrate David's birthday. After that I'll work on my talk – but that means I wouldn't have time to exercise tonight or be able to go to bed when Kristi does...

I feel tired just remembering the pressure I was under to do more all the time and to prove that I was adequate! I didn't take time to listen to the birds back then – I'll tell you that story later.

More is Better – *Or is it?*
In those days it seems I was always worrying about the things I needed to do. I kept doing more and more to compensate for feeling inadequate inside. I was governed by my ambition. The combination of my anxious pressures to prove myself to be worthy, along with my enormous capacity to for work (especially the work of ministry) made me a workaholic.[81]

You don't have to be a workaholic to have a problem with worrying about the things you need to accomplish. Perhaps you stress about having enough money or getting your errands done or finding just the right outfit or preparing a good dinner for your family. Or you might find yourself trying too hard to help someone that you're concerned about. These anxieties may push you to

---

[81] Research has shown that some people have a taste for alcohol and the capacity to drink more than most people and, therefore, are more vulnerable to become alcoholics. People like me are like that with work. If they also feel inferior or insecure then they are prone to relentlessly push themselves to achieve a sense of accomplishment. But no amount of external success ever brings the peace and confidence they long for.

overwork and miss out on being in the easy yoke of Jesus which is the source of true productivity.

Many people I talk to especially pastors, leaders, and caregivers live with the pressure to do more. What about you? What does it sound like in your head? Maybe you tell yourself things like:

"I have to prove myself"

"If I'm going to succeed it's up to me" (or "If you want something done right do it yourself")

"I can't rest till my work is done"

"I should always be doing something productive" (or "Idle hands are the devil's workshop")

"More is better" (e.g., "I have to get more done... I need more money... more clothes... more food... more exciting experiences... more people to like me...")

Thought patterns like these may drive you to accomplish more, but are they true and good?

Are You Overworking?

You may not consider yourself a "workaholic" and yet you may have some issues with working compulsively. This survey will help you to see if maybe you overwork or relate to your work in unhealthy ways. We're looking at "work" in the broad sense. Work is not just paid employment; it is also things like projects you're doing, responsibilities you have, chores you complete, volunteer service you give, and ministry you offer.

Answer each question below with "yes" (mostly true for you) or "no" (mostly *not* true for you). Then circle each "yes" answer:

- Do you find that you are able to work on a job or a project longer than most people?
- Do you keep thinking about things you're working on during free moments or while going to bed?
- When you're interrupted in the middle of a project do you get irritated?
- Do you feel restless or guilty if you're not working on something?
- Do you get so focused on your goal that you don't enjoy the process?
- Do you put yourself under pressure with self-imposed deadlines?
- When you're not accomplishing something productive do you feel inadequate?
- Do you take on more than your share of responsibility because you don't want people to think poorly of you?
- In the last six months has working long hours hurt your family or friends?
- When you fail do you feel bad about yourself?
- Do you put more thought and energy into your work than your relationships?
- Do you tend to take on more work than you have time for?
- Is your work the thing that excites you the most?
- Are you easily frustrated when you're work is not going well?
- Do you need to succeed at what you're working on to feel significant?

If you have four or more yes answers then you may be working compulsively and you may be doing this as a way of coping with unwanted emotions or unmet personal needs.

Why do we Overwork?
I have talked with many people who can't stop overworking. I understand. Sometimes I still slip back into that pattern myself. Right now I'm vulnerable to that! There's so much for me to write to you and not enough time before *Easy Yoke* needs to be in your hands. How ironic: *here I am writing to you about the easy yoke of Jesus and in danger of slipping out it myself!* So I keep reminding myself to take my own words to heart, to take breaks from writing and to pray and rest in Christ while I write.

Blaise Pascal, the great French mathematician, scientist, and Christian theologian of the 17th Century, poignantly described our problem with restless activity and overworking: "All the unhappiness of people arises from one single fact, which they cannot stay quietly in their own room."[82] Why not? Why can't we stay quietly in our own room? Why do we overwork or stay so busy even when we know better? Being preoccupied helps us to avoid feeling things that we don't want to feel. When we are still and quiet any inner distress that we are experiencing will naturally rise to the surface.

---

[82] Blaise Pascal (1623-1662), *Pensées* #136 published in 1670. Quoted in *Christianity for Modern Pagans: Pascal's Pensées* (Ignatius Press, 1993), p. 172.

We need to understand that overworking is more than just working too many hours – it's also *working for emotionally unhealthy reasons.* Most people work too much for particular seasons and may do so for good reasons. The problem is when we overwork continually and when we do our work with the pressured mindset of, "I have to prove myself." Underneath the compulsion to work are feelings of guilt, inadequacy, emptiness, or fear – fear of disapproval or fear of not having enough money. Overworking is a compensation that attempts to overcome those painful emotions.

When we overwork to prove ourselves or to feel better in some way we're relying on ourselves without the assistance of God's grace, we're trying to secure ourselves apart from God's kingdom. Always the Lord is at hand to bless, guide, and empower. But when we're determined to put our nose to the grindstone and get the work done we don't see the risen Christ there with us to direct and to help, we don't hear his words of love. Instead, we're relying only on our own intelligence and muscle, operating on the cultural message, *"I have to do more."* That's an unbiblical script for life that generates anxious overworking and renders God's grace ineffective in our lives. It's a *heavy yoke* to wear! – nothing like "walking freely and lightly" in Jesus' "unforced rhythms of grace" (Matthew 11:28-30, MSG).

The "Easy Yoke" Gospel of Jesus says to us: "You are loved and accepted by God even with your inadequacies." Relying on the grace of God sets us free – and it *sets us on fire* to love God and others!

God-Ordained Work

As we talk about overworking and the stress it creates we need to be careful that we don't get the idea that work is bad. That would be a terrible misrepresentation! By "work" I mean to refer to *whatever we do that produces something good and beneficial.* Work is necessary to life and to being in community. When God created us he commissioned us to *work.* A central part of being made in God's image is that he gave us the responsibility and *blessing* to do good for people and for all of his creation (Genesis 1:26-28). Work is God-ordained.

Did you notice that work – pulling a plow across a field to prepare it for planting – is the context of the easy yoke passage of Scripture that is our foundation text for this course?!

When Martin Luther's barber asked him about his personal pray life Luther answered him with a letter that has since become one of the treasured devotional classics: *A Simple Way to Pray.* In his letter he says something that you might not expect the great church reformer and prayer master to say: "It may well be that you may have some tasks which are as good as or better than prayer, especially in an emergency. There is a saying ascribed to St. Jerome that everything a believer does is prayer and a proverb, 'He who works faithfully prays twice.'"[83]

Indeed, one of the most obvious things about Jesus' life is that *he worked hard* – first as a carpenter and then in his

---

[83] Martin Luther (1483-1546), *A Simple Way to Pray* (Westminster John Knox Press: 2000), p. 18-19. Originally published in 1535.

public ministry. Jesus' active ministry of compassion fills the pages of the Gospels. He went from city to city preaching the Good News and engaging people in conversation about the Kingdom of God. He spoke to masses of people day and night, sometimes thousands at a time. He healed person after person that cried out for him or pushed through crowds to grab a hold of him.

For three years Jesus lived with his apprentices 24-hours a day, investing himself in The Twelve and other eager learners. He encouraged them. He served them. He answered their questions. He taught them how to live and to love. He showed them how to preach, heal, and teach. Jesus worked so hard that he said of himself, "The Son of Man has no place to rest his head" (Matthew 8:20). Frequently, crowds of needy people pressed around him and there was so much to do that he didn't even have time to eat (Mark 6:30).

And Jesus' disciples worked hard with him (before and after his resurrection) to reach as many people as they could with the Gospel that the kingdom of the heavens was available. Perhaps the best example of someone carrying on Jesus' work after his ascension is the Apostle Paul: he worked full time discipling leaders, planting churches, and ministering to people – yet he subsidized his own ministry financially by making tents (Acts 18:3). He worked hard for the Lord and he taught us to do the same:

> Our orders—backed up by the Master, Jesus—are to refuse to have anything to do with those among you who are lazy and refuse to work the way we taught you. Don't permit them to freeload on the rest. We showed you how to pull your weight when

we were with you, so get on with it. We didn't sit around on our hands expecting others to take care of us. In fact, we worked our fingers to the bone, up half the night moonlighting so you wouldn't be burdened with taking care of us. And it wasn't because we didn't have a right to your support; we did. We simply wanted to provide an example of diligence, hoping it would prove contagious.

Don't you remember the rule we had when we lived with you? "If you don't work, you don't eat." And now we're getting reports that a bunch of lazy good-for-nothings are taking advantage of you. This must not be tolerated. We command them to get to work immediately—no excuses, no arguments—and earn their own keep. Friends, don't slack off in doing your duty.

If anyone refuses to obey our clear command written in this letter, don't let him get by with it. Point out such a person and refuse to subsidize his freeloading. Maybe then he'll think twice. But don't treat him as an enemy. Sit him down and talk about the problem as someone who cares (2 Thessalonians 3:6-15, MSG).

Jesus' hard work in and through Paul and his other Apostles was so effective that it is still prospering in the lives of people like you and me over 2,000 years later!

What was Jesus' Secret?
How did Jesus have such a successful ministry? Where did he get his strength? Compassion? Wisdom? Miracle-working power? How did he deal with the overwhelming demands and stress of his ministry and yet remain *relaxed?*

Today we see some Christians, including ministry leaders, burn out, blow out with moral failures, or just "go through the motions" without much heart. Perhaps you've experienced overload from ministry or care-giving? Or you've been stressed out trying to do more than you have time for? We need to learn from Jesus. He had far more responsibility and time pressure than you or I or any human being has ever had and yet he remained unhurried, relaxed, joyful, and generous with people. How did Jesus do this?

We tend to explain Jesus' holiness and miracles by saying, "He was the Son of God." That is a fact, but it is not an adequate answer! Jesus was fully God, but he was also fully man. The secret of Jesus' peace and power was not that he was the Son of God. It was what we keep talking about in this course: *he learned to live in the easy yoke of the Father.* Remember, the Bible says, "Jesus grew in wisdom, stature, and favor with God and man" (Luke 2:52) and "He learned obedience from what he suffered" (Hebrews 5:8). What a mystery that our sinless Savior *grew* in grace and *learned* to obey God!

Jesus learned and grew in the context of his relationship of abiding in the Father's love. His time with Abba was the most important thing to him – not his ministry to others. It was Jesus' rich life of quiet prayer and tender intimacy with Abba that was the source of his love, wisdom, and power. His ministry was an *overflow* of his oneness with the Father. As he did his work he was united to the Father, so much so that when someone needed healing or something else from him usually he did stop to offer an explicit verbal prayer. For Jesus prayer and activity were always integrated.

In other words, the secret of Jesus' effective, joyful work was the *way* he worked. (Recall our discussion last chapter about Jesus' way.) Jesus did his work – and lived his whole life – in the way of God's original intention in the Garden of Eden, before the fall, submitted to and in union with God. So for Jesus his work was "no sweat."

Many Christians make the mistake of thinking that hard work is part of God's curse that came with humankind's fall into sin. But as we just said above, work actually is part of God's original intention for us in the Garden of Eden. The curse had to do with *working in the wrong way.* When God created us he designed us to work by relying on his leadership and blessing, but under the curse *we work "by the sweat of our brow"!* (Genesis 1:26-28, 3:19). Sadly, as I have done myself, many Christians tend to make their decisions and carry out their responsibilities more by the sweat of their brow than by the Holy Spirit. It is to us that Jesus says, "Come to me... My yoke is easy... My burden is light... Learn to do your work with me and in my way without sweating or stressing" (Matthew 11:28-30, paraphrase).

As a Branch Abiding in the Vine
Jesus taught us to follow his way of life and work, which he said is to be as branches abiding in a grapevine that is tended to by a gardener. The sap from the vine flows into the branches and they bear clusters of juicy grapes. Jesus himself is the Vine, the Father is the Gardener, and the Holy Spirit is the Life in the Vine (John 15:1-15).

Jesus is teaching that *the power for you and I to bear the fruit of love for others comes out of our intimate abiding in God.*

What Jesus taught he lived. He was the "Righteous Branch" (Jeremiah 23:5, 33:15) who abided in God continually. He lived a life of submission to the Father; *he only did what he saw the Father doing* (John 6:38, 12:50). So complete was his moment-by-moment reliance upon God that he knew the Holy Spirit without limit (John 3:34).

Jesus told us that the fruit in his life grew out "father and son intimacies" (Matthew 11:27, MSG). Jesus didn't have to force himself to push out fruit! It came out *naturally,* out of his abiding in the Father's love.

Jesus is confident in teaching you and I that in the midst of our stressful world we can learn to live in an "easy yoke" (Matthew 11:28-30); we can learn to live in his character and power *naturally* and *routinely.* He knows this because he proved it in his own life. Jesus was the first disciple – he was a disciple of the Father. He's gone through the process of growing in godliness and grace and so he can disciple us. In his lifestyle – in what he did and the way he did it – he shows us how to live a generous and joyous life of love for God and others.

Jesus knows from personal experience as a human being that to be "yoked" (or submitted) to God in all things was the way for you and I to live in his "unforced rhythms of grace," to walk "freely and lightly" with a smile and a hand extended to help others (Matthew 11:28-30, NIV and MSG).

The Inside – Out Flow[84]

Abide and bear fruit; it's the inside-out rhythm of life that Jesus modeled and taught. Again and again in the Gospels we see Jesus withdraw from the crowds to go and pray alone in a quiet place by the lake, in the hills, in the desert, or up in the mountains. He shared his heart with the Father. He prayed and meditated on Scripture. He listened to the Father, submitted to his leadership, and obeyed him in all things.

Jesus lived this way as a young carpenter in the quiet decades of his life in the small, obscure town of Nazareth. And he lived this way as a famous preacher in the bright lights of his public ministry.

Jesus prayed and he served. He prayed alone in quiet and he prayed in community in the synagogue or on a grassy field. He worshiped and he healed people. He meditated on Scripture and he taught astounding new insights. He fasted and he fed the hungry. He rested in quiet and he ministered in noisy crowds. He withdrew on retreat and he was patient with people who interrupted him.

Jesus is the Psalm 1 Man who meditated on the law day and night and walked in the way of righteousness and love. Jesus is the Psalm 1 Tree planted by the stream of Living Water, roots going deep into rich and moist soil, strong to survive desert drought and heat without its leaves wilting, and thus bearing fruit in season. Jesus taught us to

---

[84] Fourteen times in *The Message* paraphrase of the Bible Eugene Peterson uses this phrase "inside out."

follow his example and become good, fruit-bearing trees like him (Matthew 7:17-19; 12:33; Luke 13:6-8).

Jesus' Rhythm in the Gospel of Mark

The Gospel of Mark highlights Jesus' inside-out rhythm of life.[85] Nine times Mark gives examples of Jesus going on spiritual retreat, either alone with the Father or joined by his disciples. And after each nourishing time of abiding with the Father Jesus bore tremendous fruit for the kingdom. He received guidance and power from the Father in these spiritual retreats, which helped him to make wise ministry decisions, feed and heal thousands, and apprentice leaders to follow his ways of love.

An outline from Mark's Gospel shows the abiding and fruit-bearing rhythm of Jesus' life:

Mark 1:9-13. Jesus went on pilgrimage to be baptized and spent forty days in the desert praying in silence, solitude, meditating on Scripture, and fasting. His spiritual disciplines connected him deeply to his Father, nourishing him and strengthening him. On this wilderness retreat he solidified his mission for his public ministry and how he would carry out ministry. He was empowered by the Father and by Scripture to overcome Satan. After his pilgrimage Jesus was ready to launch his public ministry and to start inviting people to follow him as his apprentices.

---

[85] I learned this analysis of Jesus' pattern in the Gospel of Mark from Paul Jensen's book, *Subversive Spirituality*, published by Pickwick Publications, 2009.

Mark 1:35. Early in the morning Jesus had a custom of going out to lonely places to pray. Undoubtedly, his prayer times included meditating on passages from the Psalms and the prophets that he had memorized. In this instance, his prayer time gave him discernment from God that it was time to leave Capernaum and go minister in Galilee.

Mark 1:45. Jesus went out to lonely places to pray. And people came to him for ministry. (Later, in Luke 11:1-4 when the disciples saw the priority of Jesus' private prayer times, his affectionate intimacy with the God he called "Abba," and the power and glory that came from him as a result of his connection to the Father, they cried out, "Lord, teach us to pray!" And so he taught them *how* he prayed in the Lord's Prayer.)

Mark 3:13. Jesus went alone to a mountainside to pray all night. Then with guidance from the Father he gathered and appointed his 12 apostles.

Mark 6:30-32. Jesus went out on a retreat with his disciples by boat. John the Baptist died and they needed to grieve together and comfort one another. And the disciples had just finished a mission trip and wanted to talk with Jesus about it. But the crowds of people interrupted their retreat! You'd think that Jesus might set a boundary because he had his own needs to take care of. Certainly, we can sympathize with the disciples getting irritated with the crowds at this point! But Jesus' regular patterns of abiding in prayer provided a deep storehouse of grace that he could tap into in times of stress like this. Jesus patiently and generously ministered to the people. Miraculously, he fed 5,000 men (and many more women and children) with just five loaves and two fishes.

Mark 6:45-46. Jesus went up to a mountainside to walk and pray in the quiet solitude and beauty of nature. From a distance he saw his disciples in their boat on the Sea of Galilee caught in a storm. In God's power Jesus went out to them, walking on the water!

Mark 9:2-13. Jesus took Peter, James, and John to climb a mountain for a spiritual retreat. They were renewed in the beauty of nature. They talked. They prayed. They rested on the mountaintop. Then Jesus went out a ways from the three disciples, perhaps a hundred feet, so that he could abide in prayer. And suddenly right before their eyes Jesus engaged in conversation with Moses and Elijah and he was transfigured so that they saw his glory radiate like the sun! Jesus showed the disciples his divine nature as the Son of God and it changed their lives *and ours* forever! We see Jesus' glory and we know that his connection to the Father is the source of our life and transformation.

Mark 14:12-31. Jesus and his disciples went to the Upper Room for the Last Supper. This was more than a meal – it was a mini-retreat. There was food, drink, conversation, laughter, singing, teaching, and the sacrament of communion (the first one). This was an important time of renewal and preparation for the trials of the cross that were coming.

Mark 14:32-42. Jesus took Peter, James, and John to the Garden of Gethsemane. There in the olive grove they watched and prayed in a night vigil of preparation for the cross. The disciples fell asleep, but Jesus persisted in deep prayer. He surrendered his will to the Father over and over and over – he gathered his resolve to take on the sin of the world, to be tortured, to have Satan and all hell unleashed on him, to be crucified so he could save us, to trust the Father's love for him in all this, to rely on the Holy Spirit to raise him from the dead. He was ready! He was connected to Abba! He was Spirit-empowered!

These examples from Mark's gospel show that Jesus could not have lived a life of unhurried peace, godly wisdom, healing power, and love for everyone – much less gone to the cross and risen from the dead – without continually setting aside times for deep abiding in the love of his Abba Father. He could not have carried out his world-transforming ministry without a profound lifestyle of prayerful union with the Father.

Why the Birds Don't Worry

Jesus knows that you and I don't know how to live in his easy yoke rhythm of life with Abba. *What we do know how to do is to worry!* We worry about having enough to eat. We worry about what people think when they see us. We worry about running out of money. So we work, work, work! We worry, worry, worry! We rely on ourselves (or trying to get other people to do things for us).

Jesus' answer to our tendencies to worry and to overwork was to tell us to *look at the birds and listen.* No doubt, he did this himself and personally appreciated the birds singing so happily and beautifully as they gathered food, built their nests, and raised their young. Jesus had such a wonderful way of putting us at ease!

> Don't worry about what you can get – respond to what God is giving you right now. Don't worry

about how you look – open your eyes wide to
God's beauty and goodness that's all around you.

Don't worry about money. Don't worry about what *you*
have to do – give your full attention to what *God* is doing
in your life today.

All your worrying and overworking doesn't even add a
single hour to your day! Since you can't even do this very
little thing why worry about the rest?

Don't worry: Look at the birds! They are carefree because
your Heavenly Father cares for them. Don't you know that
you are much more valuable than birds?"

Fear not little ones. Your Father has been pleased to give you
the glorious riches of his eternal kingdom! Seek first his
kingdom and he will provide you with all that you need
(Matthew 6:25-34, Luke 12:22-34, selected verses
paraphrased).

The birds sing as they work because implicitly they trust
the Father's care! The conversation between the Robin
and the Sparrow echoes Jesus' teaching. Listen in with
Jesus:

> Said the Robin to the Sparrow:
> "I should really like to know
> Why these anxious human beings
> Rush about and worry so."

Said the Sparrow to the Robin:
'Friend, I think that it must be
That they have no Heavenly Father
Such as cares for you and me"[86]

Jesus is showing us that the birds know what most of us
don't know: *less is more.* Because the Father cares for
them each day they know to gather enough food for that
day rather than straining to fill up massive storehouses for
later. Notice how Jesus drives home his illustration with
humor, saying in essence: "My friends, relax! How many
birds do you think you are worth? Surely, you know that
are worth more to the Father than many birds!"[87]

The birds remind us that sometimes we need to do less
work and often we need to take breathers from our work.
And certainly, we need to be attentive to God before and
as we work to help us to rely on God's grace and not our
own sweat. When we carry out our responsibilities in
Jesus' easy yoke then we discover that doing less can
actually lead to accomplishing more of what is most
important! Inspired by the birds – and, of course, the Holy
Spirit! – we can sing while we work and enjoy producing
fruit for God that remains.

Centuries ago John Woolman[88] worked in Jesus' easy yoke
as a tailor. He worked hard and he did good work for his

---

[86] Elizabeth Cheney, *Streams in the Desert*, October 10th Devotional.

[87] Dallas Willard has a talk he gives, "How Many Birds are you Worth?"
This teaching has helped me to laugh and learn with Jesus!

[88] John Woolman (1720-1772) was a devout Quaker writer and
itinerant preacher throughout the American colonies. He was also a

customers and so his business grew. But he wrote in his journal that he was afraid that his prosperity would distract him from his relationship with Christ and staying responsive to divine "openings" in which he heard God's voice or sensed his presence. So he never let the demands of his business grow beyond what he needed to provide for himself and his family. He determined not to worry about money and not to overwork. Instead of expanding his tailor shop he practiced the "less is more" mentality and kept sending customers to his competitors who needed more business! How un-American! *How Christ-like!*[89]

Whistle While You Work

When my kids were little I watched "Snow White and the Seven Dwarfs" more times than I care to admit! But along with millions of other people I was inspired by Snow White whistling and singing while she worked to clean up all the messes the Seven Dwarfs left in their house:

> Just whistle while you work
> And cheerfully together we can tidy up the place.
> So hum a merry tune – it won't take long
> When there's a song to help you set the pace!

---

successful tailor. He is most famous for leading the movement to abolish slavery, though the effort did not succeed in his lifetime.

[89] I first heard this story from Ray Ortlund many years ago. It had a profound impact on me and for many years it has inspired me to be glad to refer therapy clients to other counselors wherever appropriate. Thomas Kelly references this part of John Woolman's story in *A Testament of Devotion*, p. 93-94.

In the Disney movie it is the singing of the birds that prompts Snow White to sing and then the Seven Dwarfs join it too, singing "Heigh-ho! Heigh-ho!" as they do their work of digging for diamonds in the mine.

Many times I've experienced the singing of the birds, like the angels in the heavens all around us, reminding me that it is the Lord who puts the song in our mouths by singing with love over us (Psalm 40:3, Zephaniah 3:17[90]). It's because of the Father's love for us that we don't need to worry or overwork – we can whistle while we work! We can sing in the midst of stress!

One Sabbath day I was meditating on Jesus' teaching, "Don't worry – look at the birds." I was inspired to sit down and do some bird watching while I prayed. As I looked and listened to what was going on above my head Jesus spoke to my heart about life in the kingdom of the heavens:

Don't Worry: Listen to the Birds
> Don't worry: Look at the birds;
> Trust my Father as they do,
> Feeding each day from his hand.
>
> Don't worry: Listen to the birds;
> Rest in my Word as they do,
> Sitting quietly and alone on the Branch.

---

[90] Remember Zephaniah 3:17? We referred to it earlier. It's one of the most wonderful promises for the Lord's people in the Bible! "The LORD your God is with you, he is mighty to save. He will take great delight in you, he will quiet you with his love, he will rejoice over you with singing."

Don't worry: Learn from the birds;
Sing with my angels as they do,
Harmonizing with the choruses of heaven.

Don't worry: Live like the birds;
Fly with my Spirit as they do,
Responding to the currents of my Breath.

Don't worry: Love like the birds;
Gather with my friends as they do,
Traveling in formation as my flock.

Many times like this I've had the experience of a delightful prayer poem rising up within me while I'm practicing a Sabbath. At first this surprised me. Then I realized that *when we enter God's rest he renews our souls and inspires our creativity.* This is how he frees us from anxious overworking.

Remembering that day I listened to the birds with Jesus inspires me even now as I write these words! I can picture the bench I was sitting on by the lake – ahhh! It is good to take a Sabbath rest! And I'm thankful that even this morning God helped me to calm down my compulsion to work and instead to sleep in and take extended hours to relax in his grace, pray from the Psalms, and meditate on a Gospel passage. It wasn't easy for me to set aside that time today when I feel like I have so much work to do and tomorrow I am taking a vacation day to visit my son in Santa Barbara. But once I set the boundary I found myself resting in Jesus' easy yoke and now, this afternoon, it's helping me to whistle while I work!

Spiritual Exercise: Sabbath-Keeping

Keeping a Sabbath day is the most repeated command in the Bible – and yet it is *the most neglected of the Ten Commandments by Christians today!* Just like most of the Israelites of old we dismiss Moses and the Prophets who repeatedly call us to remember the Sabbath. We believe we're okay to neglect the Sabbath because we think it's not a New Testament teaching – but it is! The Sabbath was practiced and taught by Jesus (Luke 4:16, Mark 6:1-2) and his disciples (Luke 23:56, Acts 16:13, 17:2), including those who were Gentiles (Acts 13:42-44).

What is the Sabbath? It is essentially a fast from work, but don't think of a somber, dour fast. Think *fasting is feasting on God.* The Sabbath is a celebratory day in which you do no work in order to honor the Lord and to rest in his love and be renewed by his sufficiency in your life. A Sabbath day is a day to *pray and play.*[91]

Many Christians misunderstand Jesus' teachings and actions that disrupted Sabbath-keeping. Jesus was not contradicting the importance of keeping a Sabbath rest to honor God; he was against the *legalistic, Pharisaical* Sabbath-keeping that was so prevalent in his day. And so he taught the people: "The Sabbath was made for man, not man for the Sabbath. So the Son of Man is Lord even of the Sabbath" (Mark 2:27-28). And he demonstrated his teaching – breaking the rigid, restrictive rules imposed on the Sabbath – by repeatedly healing people on the Holy Day.[92] Far from being duty or a chore he made it clear that the Sabbath was

---

[91] Eugene Peterson, *Working the Angles,* p. 74-75.

[92] For instance see Matthew 12:9-14, Luke 13:10-16, John 5:1-15.

an *opportunity* to participate in the action of God, to get into his easy yoke and interact with the grace and healing that God is offering right now (Mark 7:8-13).

Some people get hung up on which day to keep a Sabbath. The Jewish Sabbath has always been Saturday. The early Christians made Sunday the Sabbath to honor Christ's resurrection. But as Paul teaches, *any day* can be used for a Sabbath rest (Romans 14:4-6). That's a good thing, because Sunday is *not* a day that church leaders can rest!

Many people also get overwhelmed with the idea that a Sabbath should be a whole day and since that seems like more time than they can set aside they don't do anything. But it's not all or nothing. In learning any discipline we need to *start by doing what we can to connect with God's grace.* And we need to remember, as the writer to Hebrews explains, that the point of keeping a Sabbath is not to check it off our list, but to *enter God's rest for everyday living.* This is so important that he urges us:

> Since the promise of entering his rest still stands, let us be careful that none of you be found to have fallen short of it... As was said before: "Today, if you hear his voice, do not harden your hearts."...

There remains, then, a Sabbath-rest for the people of God; for anyone who enters God's rest also rests from his own work, just as God did from his. Let us, therefore, make every effort to enter that rest (Hebrews 4:1, 7, 9-11).

Keeping a Sabbath has helped me and many people I know to turn from worrying about their "to do" lists to being ruled by the peace of Christ (Colossians 3:15). To take a

Sabbath is to set aside a day (or a smaller block of time) to rest in God's provision, to stop your work and be "unproductive." Along these lines, as Psalm 127 teaches us, sometimes the best thing you can do on a Sabbath is to sleep![93] The Sabbath is a day to let go, to stop trying to control people and situations. It's a day to *focus on what God is graciously doing all around you so you can respond to him rather than depending only on your own abilities to make things happen.*

Keeping the Sabbath teaches us to trust God and enjoy him, to walk in Jesus' easy yoke not just on a Sabbath day but all the time. Sabbath is God's way to set us free from worry and anxiety, ambition and anger, even loneliness. Because in the green pastures of Good Shepherd's grace and beside his still waters we discover that it's really true: "He restores my soul!" (Psalm 23:3).

When you learn how to make use of a Sabbath rest then you discover the reality of your life in God's kingdom: *I am not alone. Everything doesn't depend on me. Things don't have to happen my way. God is with me helping me and working all things together for my good so I can be happy in Christ no matter what!*

---

[93] Psalm 127 is a great example of the importance of sleep and it's connection to Sabbath. It teaches us that getting enough sleep is a way of practicing our trust in God's provision. And it helps us to be more loving to our children and other family members and friends. This is one of the Psalms that the Israelites sang as they walked together on their pilgrimages to Jerusalem for the feasts which were multiple Sabbath days strung together.

Some Ways You Can Take a Sabbath Rest
You may not keep a weekly Sabbath day. I don't know
many people who do. Personally, I learned to practice the
Sabbath by staring small: over a period of years I went
from setting aside one day every quarter to one day per
month to one day per week. Along the way, I extended my
hours in silence and solitude from one to five or more. And
because it is difficult for me to be still in body and mind –
to not be active or studious – I do one or more things to
help me *enjoy being with Jesus as my Friend* like hiking,
being in nature, praying the Psalms, using Lectio Divina
(meditation) on a Gospel passage, journaling, or abiding in
prayer (e.g., Breath Prayers).

Sometimes my Sabbath days don't look so "spiritual."
Often I use vacation days with my family as Sabbath time.
Other times I use community retreat days for my Sabbath.
The important thing for me is to set aside my normal work
and responsibilities for a day, or at least a large chuck of a
day.

In approaching Sabbath time you also need to *start small*
and *be flexible* in your approach. Here is a range of
practical ideas for how you might practice enjoying some
Sabbath rest this week. Ask the Lord Jesus to lead you in
one or two ways of making space to enjoy to him:

Pray the Sabbath Psalm.
Psalm 92 begins with a notation: "A Psalm to be Sung on
the Lord's Day" (NLT). This little known Psalm is filled with
vibrant metaphors and presents the Sabbath as a day to

"give thanks to Yahweh" and to "play in honour of [the] Most High" (Psalm 92:1, Jerusalem Bible).[94]

Sleep in.
Most people today don't get enough sleep. One day sleep *at least* eight hours or take a nap. Jesus took naps. The monks call this "napsiodivina"! If you tend to overwork or are prone to feel guilty if you don't do what you "should" (e.g., do your devotions or "quiet time" with God) then sleep, or doing nothing, is probably the most important discipline for you because it can help you to focus on appreciating God's grace.

Abide in Prayer.
Set aside fifteen minutes or more in a quiet place to meditate deeply on my Psalm 62:1, 5 prayer: "In Christ alone my soul finds rest... Selah" (see below).

---

[94] In *Working the Angles* Eugene Peterson unpacks Psalm 92 (see p. 74-75).

The Sabbath Psalmist provides us with three metaphors showing that the parallel Sabbath actions of praying and playing are like music (verses 1-4), animals (verses 10-11), and palm trees (verses 12-14). *Music? Animals? Palm trees?* Yes! Praying and playing need the musician's combination of discipline and delight, the wild ox's unrestrained and exuberant prancing, and the palm tree's vibrant growth in the desert.

And because prayerful play and playful prayer are not meant to be detached from real-world-living the middle of the Sabbath Psalm also addresses how we overcome the problem of evil (verses 5-9).

Give away business to a competitor.
If you're employed you might follow John Woolman's example of "less is more" and refer a potential customer to someone else who needs the work and can do a good job. As you do this put your trust in God who provides abundantly for you and enjoy the extra space of time and energy.

Whistle while you work.
Reflect on my prayer poem inspired by Jesus' teaching, "Don't Worry: Listen to the Birds." Carry this into your work with prayer and with humming, whistling, or singing! Pause now and again for a breather to help you to work in Jesus' easy yoke.

Take a Sabbath day.
Set aside a day or a shorter block of time to rest. For these hours you are to do no work! Don't be busy, productive, or studious. Don't fill your time with errands. Relax. Enjoy. Let God lead you as to whether your time is more oriented toward playing or praying, being in solitude or with loved ones, but whatever you do purpose to do it with Jesus, your Soul Friend.

Breath Prayer
You can practice my "In Christ Alone" prayer to step out of placing your identity in your performance or what people think of you and step into Jesus' easy yoke of grace. Remember that 160 times in his letters the Apostle Paul shows us that our identity, meaning, and joy are *in Christ* alone! Let's enter the Sabbath rest of Jesus' Christ's embrace: "In Christ alone my soul finds rest... Selah" (inspired by Psalm 62:1,5).

Pause to take a breather now... Refresh your soul in
Christ... Form your heart around the desire to seek Christ
alone as your source in all that you do... Pray slowly, over
and over, "In Christ alone my soul finds rest... Selah."

You might try it as a Breath Prayer. Breathe in slow and
deep as you whisper or think: "In Christ alone my soul
finds rest..." Then breathe out: "Selah."

Repeat this a few times. As you breathe in focus on
trusting Christ... As you hold your breath focus on keeping
Christ in your heart... As you exhale focus on letting go of
stress... (This is a way of using your body in prayer to help
you to engage your mind.)

As in the previous chapter, try this as a "Simplifying Breath
Prayer". Put your whole heart into seeking Christ alone.
Pray one line per breath until all that you pray is, "Christ":

> In Christ alone my soul finds rest... Selah
>
> In Christ alone my soul... Selah
>
> In Christ alone... Selah
>
> In Christ... Selah
>
> Se... lah
>
> Christ...

Perhaps it would help you to connect with Christ if you
imagine being like Mary: she set aside her kitchen work
and her sister Martha's expectations and just sat at Jesus'

feet adoring him and listening to him (Luke 10:38-42). Set aside your work, your thoughts of being "productive." Set aside your concerns about what other people want you to do. If you're worried about money then set aside those burdens too. Simply enjoy being with Jesus!

If you have time you may want to extend the "In Christ" Breath Prayer. Try replacing the word "rest" with each of the five fruitful, virtuous states of being, one at a time: "faith", "hope", "love", "joy", "peace" (e.g., "In Christ alone my soul finds faith... Selah.").[95]

This will help you to cultivate a fruitful character, holy and healthy – the virtuousness of Christ! These five godly states of being are wonderfully positive, pleasant, and energizing emotions associated with them (but don't reduce them to being merely emotions!).

It's easy to memorize: "In Christ alone my soul finds rest... Selah." Then you can offer little Breath Prayers throughout the day to help you to practice God's presence. What peace will be yours! What peace you'll be able to give to the people you encounter!

Salty Questions

This week we've been discussing the daily stress of work and responsibility and the problems that we may have

---

[95] We often think of faith, hope, love, joy, and peace as feelings, maybe not faith, but certainly the other four. I'm calling them "states of being" or character traits because, as Dallas Willard explains, they include, but are much larger than, our emotions. They primarily have to do with our mindset and the orientation of our will, but they also are part of our bodies and they profoundly affect our social relations. See Renovation of the Heart (Navpress: 2002), p. 117-139).

with this. Talking with your soul friend or group about your struggles and what you're learning will help you to learn from your daily life trials (the third corner in our Triangle of Soul Tansformation). Be honest, listen well, and be prayerful and you'll find your soul talk to be spiritually salty!

What is one thing that you learned about Jesus' way of working?

Do you tend to worry or overwork? Do you feel that you need to accomplish things to prove that you're adequate or to feel better in some other way? What is an example?

How did you practice taking a Sabbath rest? What impact did it have on you?

You Can Live in Jesus' Easy Yoke: Lesson #7
You Don't Have to Walk on Eggshells!

The starter's gun was about to fire to start the triathlon. It was time for a final gut check: was I ready to dive in and face my fear of swimming a half-mile in the ocean?

I was standing on the beach with my 19-year old son and hundreds of other swimmers crammed like sardines on the beach and looking into an ocean of freezing cold water. I was shivering and I wasn't even in the water yet! Six foot high waves, one after the other, were roaring towards me and I was going to have to swim through those crashing walls of salt water and go a quarter mile out to a buoy that I could barely see and then come back to shore.

Soon all the people around me would be thrashing, kicking, and splashing into me, trying to get in front of me. But I didn't care about being first – I just wanted to finish the race alive! *Really.* I had been told that recently a shark had eaten a person on that very beach! I tried to dismiss this thought as highly unlikely. But I worried, *How am I going to breathe with all the waves and splashes of water coming into my face? What if I start choking on salt water?*

I meditated on the Apostle Paul's words:

For me to live is Christ and to die is gain...

> One thing I do... I press on toward the goal to win the prize for which God has called me heavenward in Christ Jesus...

I have learned to be content whatever the circumstances. I know what it is to be in need, and I know what it is to have plenty… I can do everything through Christ who gives me strength" (Philippians 1:21, 3:13-14, 4:13).

"I can do everything through Christ who gives me strength… I can die through Christ who gives me strength… I can overcome my fear through Christ who gives me strength… I can swim in this ocean through Christ who gives me strength…"

I "took courage" from my Lord. *Live or die* I was going to swim the roaring ocean with Jesus! I was not going to shrink back! So when the gun sounded I dove into the ocean and started swimming for my medal!

But as I swam it was obvious that *I was struggling.* I took in a lot of salt water! I felt and looked like I was dog paddling as all the expert swimmers passed me up. In fact, along the swim route there were lifeguards sitting atop surfboards and separately two of them asked me, "Are you okay?" They were afraid I was going to drown! But I was praying as I swam, "I can do everything through Christ who gives me strength." The lifeguards didn't see that I was swimming with Jesus! Nonetheless, I'm glad they were watching me closely!

And I thank God that assisted by his grace I finished the swim and my first triathlon. How did I do? For the swimming portion I came in 70th place out of 72 male swimmers my age! I did a lot better on the bike and the run, but beating other people was not the point – it was about diving in to face my fear with Jesus.

Angelica was Afraid to Upset her Husband

"As soon as my husband comes through the door after work I start walking on eggshells," Angelica told me. "I try so hard to make him happy, but still he gets mad at me: dinner is late, the kids didn't pick up their toys, I talk too long on the phone with my mother, or maybe he just had a bad day at the office – it's always something."

Angelica was the sweetest person you could ever meet – so friendly and pleasant to everyone, including her husband. But I knew how she felt inside. She continually complained to me about how difficult her husband was to live with. The truth was that *she was angry at him* for being preoccupied with his work, having impossible expectations of her and the kids, and saying many hurtful things to her over the years.

But Angelica was afraid to tell *him* that she was angry. "That'd just make things worse!" she insisted to me. She didn't want even to admit that she was mad at him because it wasn't "nice" and she hated conflict. She couldn't bear to disappoint her husband and "make" him angry so she was tense and anxious all the time about pleasing him. Even when he was happy with her she worried because she knew that sooner or later he'd find fault with her. And then when he did criticize her she'd keep quiet and tolerate it to avoid an argument. She even clamed up when he spoke harshly with the kids, which she felt terrible about, but that's how afraid she was of his anger and how insecure she felt inside.

It was important to Angelica to be an honest person, but because it was so upsetting to her when she got into an argument with her husband she sometimes hid things from him or told him "white lies." For instance, he tried to keep her on a real tight budget and it was hard for her stay within this especially when it came to their children. So when she "splurged" and spent money on new outfits for the kids she tried to keep it from him. Usually he didn't notice, but when he did she'd make up a story and say that her mother bought the clothes for them.

Of course, despite her efforts to "keep the peace", sometimes her husband did get mad at her and sometimes she lost her temper too and then whether it was him, her, or both of them who got angry she'd feel hurt and abandoned. Then she'd blame herself and feel guilty. And then she'd re-double her hyper-vigilant efforts to anticipate everything he wanted and do it for him so there wouldn't be any more conflict. The cycle was exhausting!

Angelica walked on eggshells with other people too, but it was the worst with her husband. Despite the stress of carrying all that anxiety and guilt inside her Angelica did not want to face her fear of talking to her husband about how she felt in their relationship – that was an ocean she did not want to dive into!

Trying to Make People Happy
Angelica believed that she was responsible to *make* her husband and other people happy. Doing whatever she could to please people was how she showed her love. She maintained, "It's my Christian duty to do all that I can to make people happy – it'd be *selfish* not to help people and just think about what I want." And as long as she helped people, pleased them, and avoided conflict with them then she felt secure and confident. But if not then she felt anxious and guilty. She was a "mood matcher" so the only

way she knew to be happy was to make her loved ones happy.

People like Angelica live by what they believe are altruistic motives like...
"I need to make people happy" ("I should always be nice so I don't hurt people's feelings")
"I have to deny myself and care for other people"
"It's selfish to think of my own needs"
"When I see someone has a problem I should always try to fix it"

Caring for other people and helping them are essential expressions of love and this is what Angelica thought she was doing. She believed she was following the teachings of the Bible when she disregarded herself and put all her energy into making her husband happy or fixing his problems.

But her life was filled with anxiety and fear. She didn't know how to walk in Jesus' easy yoke for her because she didn't have good personal boundaries.

How are Your Boundaries?
Maybe you relate to Angelica's fear of displeasing other people? Or the pressure to avoid conflicts? Or feeling guilty when someone is angry with you? These are boundary issues.

The *Boundaries Survey* can help you to assess if you may need to work on strengthening your boundaries in your relationships. Answer each question below with "yes" (mostly true for you) or "no" (mostly *not* true for you). Then circle each "yes" answer.

- Do you tolerate mistreatment from people in hopes of being loved?
- Do you depend on people who are emotionally unavailable to care for you?
- Do you feel compelled to help people to feel better or to solve their problems?
- Do you rescue others from the consequences of their irresponsible behavior?
- Do you feel empty, bored, or unimportant if you're not helping someone or responding to a crisis?
- Is it hard for you to say "no" when someone asks you for help?
- Is it hard for you to ask for help?
- In close relationships do you lose interest in your own hopes and desires?
- Are you quick to get angry about injustices done to others?
- Do you often talk about other people and their problems?
- Do you worry about how other people are feeling?
- Do you worry about other people's opinions of you?
- Do you keep quiet to avoid conflicts with people?
- Is it hard for you to disagree with a boss or someone else in authority?
- Do you hide things or tell "white lies" to avoid upsetting people?
- Do you feel more comfortable giving to others rather than receiving from them?
- Is it difficult for you to receive attention, compliments, or gifts from others?

The questions you answered "yes" to indicate an area of struggle with maintaining your separate identity and well-being in the context of a relationship. If you have five or more yes answers, of if you answered yes to any question that is very painful or problematic for you, then you probably need help strengthening your personal boundaries and your sense of self.

Boundaries[96]

Jesus taught us, "Simply let your 'Yes' be 'Yes,' and your 'No,' 'No'" because trying to get people to do the things you want or trying to get them to think well of you is manipulative and "comes from the evil one" (Matthew 5:37). Jesus is telling us not to be manipulative or evasive, but to be direct and honest with people. The abilities to say yes and no and to speak the truth in love are examples of personal boundaries.

Your "boundaries" are what define your identity. Imagine your person like a home. You have a yard with a fence designating your property line. You have a gate at the entrance to your sidewalk and a front door to your house that locks. Inside your house is an entry way, living room, kitchen and family room, and your personal bedroom.

To have good boundaries begins with being *aware* of what is in each area and room and be able to talk about it. Essentially, setting a boundary is expressing yourself – your thoughts (including your beliefs and values), feelings,

---

[96] *Boundaries* by Dr.'s Henry Cloud and John Townsend is a best-selling (and most helpful!) book on this subject. They integrate Bible and psychology and offer many practical examples of how to develop good personal boundaries.

choices, body (including your physical needs and gifts), relationships, and soul (including your deep longings and needs) that make up your unique personality.[97] Being self-aware is always good and helpful. When you knowing what is important to you then you can communicate that to others and direct your actions in godly ways.

Boundaries relate to trust, the capacity to open and close your door (say yes or no) and the discernment to know when to do which. Most anyone can stand at your gate outside your house, but not many people are invited all the way into your bedroom. At your home you open or close the door to someone depending upon how much you trust him or her. When you have strong boundaries you are able to say yes and let good into your personal space and you are able to say no to keep bad out. You are free to say yes or no as it relates to doing things for people. The abilities to say yes and no go together. For instance, when a difficult person wants to talk with you if you're confident in your ability to end the conversation when you need to do so (say no) then you'll be free to begin the conversation (say yes). If you're not confident you can say no then your only recourse to avoid being smothered is to run when you see the person!

Having boundaries is an essential aspect of the image of God in us. God has boundaries; he is three Persons in One and there are ways that he is separate from us. The often repeated Biblical words of "Be holy because I, the LORD your God, am holy" (Leviticus 19:2) are an example of God

---

[97] These are the parts of a person's identity that Dallas Willard discusses at length *Renovation of the Heart* (Navpress, 2002).

expressing his identity and calling us to rely on him to help us to become like him. The Bible is full God expressing his identity – "I am _____" – and affirming our identity – "You are _____."

Having good boundaries – self-awareness, personal responsibility, and the ability to say yes or no – is the basis of empathy, love, initiative, and motivation. Personal soul care, ministry to other people, capacity to do good work, and love for God are each dramatically impacted by how mature your boundaries are. The stronger your boundaries, the freer you are to make choices, including to step into Jesus' easy yoke, doing all that you do with him in his kingdom and for him and his glory.

The Eggshells Always Break!

Have you ever tried to walk on eggshells without breaking any? *It's impossible!* And it's so stressful. But I've talked to many men and women like Angelica who are determined to try. They have problems with their boundaries. They tend to match other people's moods. They don't know how to be happy if their loved one is grumpy or to be at peace if their loved one is stressed; they haven't learned to maintain a separate sense of self and personal well being in the context of their relationships.

Caregivers and people in ministry are especially prone to get tied into relationships with people who are needy, dysfunctional, abusive, addicted, or just difficult. This problem is called codependency.[98] Codependents have a

---

[98] "Co-dependency" is a term that emerged in the 1980's from the treatment of alcoholics. It was found that alcoholics typically had at least one person in their lives that unwittingly served to "enable" them to drink irresponsibly without suffering many of the negative

pattern of enmeshing with people who have an addiction or other life problem and trying to help them and be accepted by them. Inside they are afraid to be their true self and be rejected, but instead of admitting that they divert the focus to the person they're in relationship with.

Codependents like Angelica minimize or deny their emotions. Consciously, Angelica was always worrying about what other people felt: her husband, mother, kids, friends, sister, whoever. In fact, when I asked her how she felt in her marriage invariably she answered by telling me her *perceptions* of what her husband was going through:

"He's frustrated with his boss… He came home grumpy again… He doesn't like it when I cook healthy foods… He wants our kids to be more responsible, but he keeps falling behind on paying our bills… It seems like he's never happy with the kids or me… He can be real jerk…"

But *unconsciously,* underneath her perceptions of her husband, she had her own painful emotions and desires that she didn't want to admit to. But if she were more emotionally aware and personally responsible then she'd invite me into her heart like this:

---

consequences of their behavior. Co-dependents can develop their own addiction. They get enmeshed with the addict in their lives, deny their own needs and emotions, become emotionally intertwined with the addict, pay the price for the addicts dysfunctional behavior, and compulsively try to fix the irresponsible person's addition and other problems.

There are helpful recovery groups for codependents like Al-Anon, Codependents Anonymous, and Celebrate Recovery, which is a Christian program offered by many churches.

"I'm afraid he's going to lose his job... It depresses me when he comes home stressed... I want our kids to be free to play and have fun at home and not have to worry about constantly picking up their toys... I'm angry that he doesn't help me more with the kids... I feel hurt when he doesn't like the dinner I made... I'm tired of trying so hard to please him... I feel so alone, like he doesn't really know me..."

Another issue is that Angelica expected her husband to do for her what she was trying to do for him: *make her happy!* Her boundaries were crisscrossed – she tried to make him happy and he was supposed to make her happy. She wasn't aware of it, but she was putting responsibility for her emotional well being on her husband. It was up to him to make her feel good about herself by giving her attention. It was up to him to help her feel good by coming home in a good mood. She wasn't taking responsibility for her own needs. And she was emotionally depending on someone who she didn't feel safe with. This reinforced her insecurity and fear.

As we've said earlier, anxiety is a symptom of trying to control people and situations and Angelica was doing a lot of that! She didn't realize it, but she was trying to control her husband to avoid conflict with him and maintain her own fragile sense of peace when she:
Did whatever she thought her husband wanted
Told "white lies" if she had don't something that he wouldn't like

Was nice to her husband's face, but then talked bad about him behind his back to her mother and other people[99]
Nagged him and gave unsolicited advice to help him be a better man
Blamed herself for making him upset

But these behaviors just made her problems worse because she was enabling him to be irresponsible and inconsiderate and she was perpetuating her anxiety.

At bottom Angelica's problem was that she wasn't living in the kingdom of God, she was living in the kingdom of her husband. Actually, it'd be more true to say that she was living in the kingdom of Angelica: *instead of submitting to the Lord and finding her sufficiency in him she was relying on her own abilities to make herself happy by making her husband and other people happy.*

What the Bible Actually Teaches
"The make people happy" messages are *unhappy* narratives for life that generate a lot of pressure, guilt, and frustration. They may seem to be supported by the Bible, but careful Bible study shows that at most they are half-truths. They are among the "Biblical Blunders that Bruise and Confuse" that I referenced previously.[100] In contrast to these false narratives the Bible teaches:

---

[99] Gossip and slander are boundary violations of others. Jesus teaches us to go directly to the person who has offended us and talk the issue through privately. Then if that doesn't work we're to bring someone along to help us resolve the conflict (Matthew 18:15-17).

[100] For more Biblical insights read "Recovery from Codependency," my compilation of Bible Verses on SoulShepherding.org.

Sometimes Love Hurts.
Love is not always nice; it does not always make people feel good. I like to say, "There are two words for love: yes and no (see Matthew 5:37). Jesus shows us this, as he does not always do what people want him to do. In succinct words, Paul gave us God's wisdom for growing up in Christ when he said, "speak the truth in love" (Ephesians 4:15). And in the Gospels Jesus shows us the perfect integration of grace and truth (John 1:14, 17).

Godly Self-Denial Comes from a Loved Person.
Certainly, Jesus teaches us to deny ourselves in order to follow him in a life of love (Luke 9:23-25). But he also teaches us to love our neighbor *as we love ourselves* (Mark 12:29-31). Similarly, Paul teaches us to look out for other people's interests even as it would be natural and healthy to look out for our own interests (Philippians 2:4). He teaches that we're to put off our "old self" and put on our "new self" (Ephesians 4:22-24, Colossians 3:9-10). God would not want us to disregard our new, redeemed self! And the psychological reality is that we cannot deny a "self" (our identity and personhood) that we haven't developed! When we have sufficient awareness and appreciation of the self that God is making us into and we have the capacity for appropriate self-care and self-esteem then we can set aside our own needs for the moment and be generous with others.

There is a Good "Selfishness."
Jesus instructed us to ask for what we need. He put petition in the middle of the Lord's Prayer and he also told us to keep asking for what we need because God is our loving Father (Matthew 6:9-13, 7:7-11). The truth is that

it's more selfish *not* to ask people for what you need because if you don't then the people who love you will be burdened with trying to figure out what you need and finding a way to care for you, despite your resistances. As Angelica's case illustrated, it's simply inhuman and not even possible to live without having needs so if you try to do so you'll just be repressing them and they'll unconsciously affect your behavior in ways that confuse, burden, manipulate, or violate others. That's the kind of selfishness that's a problem!

Don't Do for People what They Need to Do.
Normally, it is not helpful to rescue people from the painful consequences of their actions. This enables them to continue their problem behavior because it removes their natural incentive to take responsibility for themselves and to make personal changes. Even in Jesus' healing ministry he always gave people something to do, some way to participate in their physical healing. There was a problem with rescuing and responsibility in the church at Galatia and Paul taught them the balance: "Carry each other's burdens, and in this way you will fulfill the law of Christ... *For each one should carry his own load*" (Galatians 6:2, 5, italics added).

Adult Children and their Mothers
For many adults the hardest person for them to have good boundaries with is their mother. And this is not because mothers are intrusive, judgmental, or controlling! Of course, some mothers, even those who are well intentioned, may have problems overriding the personal boundaries of their children. But the more typical problem in mother and adult child relationships is actually one of closeness.

Every person needs to be bonded with someone who is warm and nurturing, validates our emotions and needs, and appreciates our unique personality. And our primary source for this grace-giving, especially early in life, is our mothers. And yet our need to be attached in caring relationship is in tension with our need to be separate and to express our individuality. It may feel like meeting one need comprises the other. And for our mother she may feel smothered by our needs for care or rejected by our needs for individuation. This push-pull can be difficult even in healthy family relations!

God's purpose in the mothering that children receive is that they would be able to pray with thanks to the Lord as David did: "You brought me out of the womb; you made me trust in you even at my mother's breast" (Psalm 22:9). Like David, Paul's disciple Timothy experienced nurture and encouragement that was central to the growth of his faith in the Lord (2 Timothy 1:5).

Of course, as we said in an earlier lesson, sometimes even as adults we need personal healing and substitute mothering to get to that point of trust in the goodness of God at all times and in all situations. In any case, we all need a few people (at least one!) that we can trust and respect to be "Christ's Ambassadors" who represent and mediate God's love to us (2 Corinthians 5:20). In the Body of Christ we are to "love one another" – we are, as best we can, to be as Christ to one another.

Grace-giving and truth-revealing relationships with people support the ministry of the Holy Spirit and the Word of God in our lives to that we appreciate with the Apostle

John that, "The Word became flesh and made his dwelling among us. We have seen his glory, the glory of the One and Only, who came from the Father, full of grace and truth" (John 1:14). Jesus Christ came is the perfect integration of grace and truth – relational connection and structured boundaries – that meets our needs for bonding and for boundaries. We come to know the grace and truth of Christ through the Holy Spirit and the Bible.

Jesus' Boundaries with Mary
Jesus' relationship with his mother Mary is a great example of how love and boundaries belong together. Have you ever noticed this?

Mary demonstrates for us the posture of submission to and reliance upon God that we need in all that we do. Really, she offers the *perfect prayer* when she responds to angel's announcement that she was to participate in the immaculate conception of the Messiah and Son of God by praying: "Let it be to me according to your word" (Luke 1:38, NKJV). And she stood with John at the foot of the cross, they being the only two of all of Jesus' family, friends, and followers to remain faithful to him through the sufferings of his crucifixion.

But in between these two shining examples of faith we see that Mary has some personal struggles, particularly in her relationship with Jesus, such that Jesus needs to set boundaries with her. As with all of our Bible heroes, we can be thankful that Mary in her humanity provides us a realistic role model – not only can we look up to her, but also we can relate to her weaknesses and this helps us to rely on God's grace to become more like her.

When Jesus was twelve years old she and Joseph took him on a spiritual pilgrimage to Jerusalem. It's hard to believe in our society today, but this was a rite of passage into spiritual adulthood for Jesus. And when he was in Jerusalem he went off on his own to go the temple and there he interacted with the religious leaders in deep conversation about the Holy Scriptures and he astounded them all with his wisdom. Mary did not know where Jesus was and after a few days she understandably became quite worried and upset. When she finally found Jesus she blurted out: "Young man! Why have you treated us like this? Your father and I have been worried sick looking all over Jerusalem trying to find you!" (Luke 2:48, paraphrase).

Jesus responded: "Why were you so anxious and searching for me? You should have known that I'd be in my Father's house doing his work" (Luke 2:49, paraphrase). Notice that Jesus does not take responsibility for Mary being upset with him – he doesn't feel bad or guilty. Nor does he react with anger at her apparent guilt trip. In fact, we read: "Then Jesus went down to Nazareth with them and was obedient to them" (Luke 2:51).

How did Jesus remain so calm, so secure, so loving? Where did this young man get the presence of mind to speak the truth in love so clearly and respectfully in the midst of a very stressful situation in which he was being tested in intense, adult discussions with learned Scribes and Pharisees and was suddenly interrupted by a scolding from his Mommy? The answer is the critical point that we keep coming back to: *Jesus was in the easy yoke, standing in the invisible kingdom of his Father who loved him.* He was able to maintain a separate emotional grounding from Mary's frustration, the religious leaders' opinions of him, and the overall stress of the moment because his intimacy with Abba provided him with the compassion, respect, and confidence that he needed.

Jesus demonstrated the same healthy boundaries years later when he was beginning his public ministry. He was at the Cana wedding with Mary and she pressured him to fix the problem that her friends who were hosting the wedding party had run out of wine. He calmly and matter of factly set a limit with her and told her that this was not his problem. But then in secret he went ahead and miraculously changed the water into wine to bless the host and wedding party and, more importantly, to reveal his glory to his disciples (John 2:1-11).

Then not long after wedding at Cana when Jesus was at the height of his popularity and he was ministering in a house that was jam-packed, overflowing with people his boundaries were again tested. His mother and brothers heard about the situation and "they went to take charge of him, for they said, 'He is out of his mind.'" Perhaps they wanted to take Jesus back to Nazareth to their family home and carpenter's shop. But once again, Jesus did not let Mary's (or his siblings') emotions or desires *define or control him*. Again, he spoke the truth in love and said no, insisting that he was going to stay in the house and continue teaching the people and healing those who were sick – as long as the Father directed him (Mark 3:20-35).

Jesus Set Boundaries in his Helping [101]
The way Jesus was with Mary is the way he was with everyone he ministered to. He never walked on eggshells around people, worrying about upsetting them, clinging to them for approval, or pushing to get them to do what they should. He was self-aware, secure, solid, purposeful, straightforward, loving. The Gospels are full of examples of that Jesus:

Accepted the physical limitations of 24 hours in a day, being in one place at a time, and having just three years of public ministry to work with

Set boundaries on inappropriate behavior

Disagreed with the Pharisees and other authority figures

Spoke the truth in love

Walked away from entire villages of needy people when the Father said it was time to go to another place

Walked away from hateful crowds that wanted to stone him or throw him off of a cliff

Walked away from applauding crowds that wanted to make him a spectacle, political king, or miracle worker on demand

Withdrew from people to pray

Said yes to his closest friends and no to his other friends, taking only Peter, James, and John on retreat with him

Said no to his closest friends

Had expectations for everyone he helped that they do their part in order to be healed or to make a life change

If Jesus had not been able to set boundaries like these then he would not have been able to be completely

---

[101] See "Jesus Set Boundaries in his Helping," my compilation of Bible Verses on SoulShepherding.org.

devoted to the Father and his life mission. Because he could say no to lesser things he was able to say yes to what was best. Once again we see that Jesus lived in the same easy yoke that he offers to us.

Live with Christ as your Center
Thomas Kelly, a Quaker missionary and teacher of the early 20th Century, experienced a great spiritual renewal after asking his spiritual friends to join him in a small group in which they read and prayed from the classic books of Christian devotion. He writes about the importance of "living from a Center, a divine Center."[102] He says that we need to become "skilled in the inner life, where the real roots of our problem lie."[103] He urges us to simplify and focus our lives on Christ. He gives us another way of describing the easy yoke of living with Christ-like boundaries:

The outer distractions of our interests reflect an inner lack of integration of our own lives. We are trying to be several selves at once, without all our selves being organized by a single, mastering Life within us. Each of us tends to be, not a single self, but a whole committee of selves... It is as if we have a chairman of our committee of the many selves within us, who does not integrate the many into one but who merely counts the votes at each decision...

And we are unhappy, uneasy, strained, oppressed, and fearful we shall be shallow. For over the margins of life

---

[102] *A Testament of Devotion,* written by Thomas Kelly (HarperCollins, 1941), p. 93.

[103] *A Testament of Devotion,* p. 91.

comes a whisper, a faint call, a premonition of richer living which we know we are passing by. Strained by the very mad pace of our daily outer burdens, we are further strained by an inward uneasiness, because we have hints that there is a way of life vastly richer and deeper than all this hurried existence, a life of unhurried serenity and peace and power. If only we could slip over into that Center! If only we could find the Silence which is the source of sound!

We have seen and known some people who seem to have found this deep Center of living, where the fretful calls of life are integrated, where No as well as Yes can be said with confidence. We've seen such lives, integrated, unworried by the tangles of close decisions, unhurried, cheery, fresh, and positive. These are not people of dallying idleness nor of obviously mooning meditation; they are busy carrying their full load as well as we, but without any chafing of the shoulders with the burden, with quiet joy and springing step. Surrounding the trifles of their daily life is an aura of infinite peace and power and joy...

Let me talk very intimately and very earnestly with you about Him who is dearer than life. Do you really want to live your lives, every moment of your lives, in His Presence? Do you long for Him, crave Him? Do you love His Presence? Does every drop of blood in your body love Him? Does every breath you draw breathe a prayer, a praise to Him? Do you sing and dance within yourselves, as you glory in His love? Have you set yourselves to be His, and *only* His, walking every moment in holy obedience?

If you say you haven't the time to go down into the recreating silences, I can only say to you, 'Then you don't *really* want to, you don't yet love God above all else in the world, with all your heart and soul and mind and strength.' ...We find time for what we *really want* to do. [104]

The Psalm 1 Man

Jesus invites us to get into his position of strong boundaries, which is to say that he invites us into the easy yoke with him to live in the kingdom of the heavens as his apprentice. As we touched on in a previous chapter, Psalm 1 gives us a vibrant picture of this life with God. Jesus is the perfect Psalm 1 Man and he offers to teach us to become like him.

The Psalm 1 Man rejects worldly counsel and sinful ways to delight in and meditate on the law of God – the Word or message of God's loving purposes for us – day and night. "He is like a tree planted by streams of water, which yields its fruit in season and whose leaf does not wither. Whatever he does prospers" (Psalm 1:3). Let's relate this metaphor to the situations that stress our personal boundaries.

If you're a Psalm 1 man or woman like Jesus when some offends you, pressures you, or is upset at you it doesn't define you or cause you to react negatively. Through your meditations and prayers you already have been permeating yourself with God's Word, rooting into his love, and drawing up nourishment from the rivers of the Holy Spirit. Then when you come into a situation in which

---

[104] *A Testament of Devotion,* p. 91-92, 95, 96.

someone says or does something hurtful you are not so distressed by it. Even under the pressure of sweltering heat and drought your leaves stay green and you have the capacity to bear fruit because your roots go down deep to the stream of life; even when people are offensive you don't internalize it to become wounded or ashamed by it, but remain separate and secure in your personal boundaries, rooted in God's kingdom, and therefore able to bear the fruit of love even for those mean people. You are defined or controlled by the visible landscape of conflict but by the invisible landscape of the glorious kingdom of the heavens.

How Angelica Simplified Her Life
Angelica became more aware of her emotions, took ownership of them, and took courage so that when it was an appropriate time she would verbalize her feelings and desires to her husband. Sometimes this meant asking him for something she needed, like help with the kids or cleaning up after dinner or time for the two of them to talk without interruption. Other times it meant speaking the truth in love to him (rather than being evasive or dishonest), by telling him that she felt hurt and angry when he didn't show appreciation the work she put into dinner or by directly asking him when she felt it was time to get new clothes for the kids.

Also when her husband asked her to do something out of the ordinary like having his mother stay in their home for two weeks or changing churches because he was frustrated with the pastor she didn't just automatically say yes. Instead, she'd talk it over with him and then say, "Let me pray about that and get back to you." Separating herself from the pressure to please him on the spot and buying time to pray and to get more perspective helped her to re-ground herself in the kingdom of Love and to be able to say no when God guided her in that way.

Another example of Angelica simplifying her life by setting a boundary was in her house cleaning. Previously she accepted her husband's pressure to keep the house immaculate. She learned that this was about *his perfectionism* and that it wasn't her responsibility to accommodate that or to make him happy. In other words, she stopped enabling his bad behavior. Of course, it wouldn't be right for her to go to the opposite extreme and leave the house a mess all the time just to spite him! But she found a balance of keeping their home clean and orderly and asking her husband and kids to help out.

Angelica was able to stop walking on eggshells in these ways because she took hold of Jesus' hand and learned to live in terms of the kingdom of God, rather than her ability to please her husband. With practice over time she found that being yoked to Jesus was a lot easier and better than being yoked to her husband's emotions! She simplified her life before Christ and was free to give her heart to him as her Lord.

Spiritual Exercise: Setting Boundaries

We practice spiritual disciplines because it's only by applying God's wisdom to our particular life situations that we learn and grow. We don't become more like Jesus merely by reading or studying (as important as these spiritual disciplines are) but by holding Christ's hand as we step out into the unknown, trying something new with our gracious Lord.

Joshua says to us, "Choose for yourselves this day whom you will serve... But as for me and my household, we will serve the LORD" (Joshua 24:15). Your opportunity this week is choose to serve the Lord by practicing setting boundaries in a relationship that is dysfunctional or is causing undo stress. To say no simplifies your life and frees up more space and energy so that you can be more devoted to the Lord.

To express personal limitations that may be unpopular with some people requires that you trust the sufficiency of God for yourself and for others. The Psalmist prays,

> God is my refuge and strength, an ever-present help in trouble... You are my portion, O Lord... You are a shield all around me, O Lord; you bestow glory on me and lift up my head... [You] brought me out into a spacious place... The boundary lines have fallen in pleasant places for me (Psalm 46:1, 119:57, 3:3, 18:19, 16:6).

The Psalmist is inviting us to follow his example of learning to be secure and happy in God's kingdom even as we are dealing with conflict, mistreatment, or high stress. He is saying that the presence of his Lord and King in his life is all that we truly need. As we said earlier in this chapter, we can learn with the Psalmist to be like the tree planted by the stream that doesn't have to force out fruit (e.g., accommodate whatever they want from you, take responsibility to solve their problems, do what you "should" to look good in others' eyes) because it grows naturally in season as it remains rooted in God.

Setting boundaries can be more than a psychological tool –
it can also be a spiritual discipline that helps to establish
further your self-identity in Christ and his kingdom of light
and love. By saying no to straining to make people happy
or fix them we can yes to Christ's rule in our lives and in
other people's lives. (And it's also true that saying yes to
Christ in new and deeper ways gives us added strength to
say no, even if setting that limit might escalate tensions or
disappoint someone.)

Oftentimes, to set a boundary requires that you let go of a
way that you have felt (or tried to feel) in control of things
through seeking approval from people, being nice and
sweet, getting something done "right," or being helpful. If
you're used to doing these things then relinquishing your
perceived control will probably increase your anxiety at
first. But it's only by facing our fears (e.g., swimming in the
ocean) that we can overcome them.

By living within your personal limitations you can venture
on God to see what he'll do when you make more space
for him to act in your life and in the relationship you're
concerned about. You're putting God to the test to see if
over time you don't discover that it's really true: Jesus'
yoke is easy – *for you and for the person(s) you're having
difficulty with!*

Some Ways You Might Set Boundaries
Ask God to show you one relationship in which you're
walking on eggshells, getting enmeshed, taking on too
much responsibility. Consider before the Lord what it
might look like for you to set a limit in order to make more
space, time, or energy for your relationship with Christ.

Practice saying no this week with one or two of these exercises for strengthening your boundary muscles:

Don't Deny your Emotions.
Have you been repressing feelings of being hurt or pressured by someone? Or have you been hiding things to avoid conflict? Instead of internalizing stress to keep peace tell your friend or family member how you feel. You need to learn to accept the reality of your emotions (emotions themselves are not sinful), think about them, and choose godly dispositions and behavior. When you do communicate your emotions of hurt or anger to someone, be careful not to be critical or blaming! Instead, take the posture that you are simply *inviting this person to understand your experience and personal needs.*

Don't Depend on Unsafe People.
Are you emotionally depending on a person for approval who in hindsight is not a good Christ's Ambassador for you? It's important to limit your vulnerability to the people that its wise for you trust and respect. This week when you are tempted to seek approval from this unsafe person instead go directly to Christ in prayer or talk with a friend you respect who helps you to trust in God's grace.

Don't Be the Hero!
Do you feel pressure to be super-responsible about something when there is someone else who could also be involved to help? Wait before you jump in to be the hero – trust Jesus Christ to be the Savior! And give someone else a chance to be used by God or ask for someone to help you and thank the Lord that success isn't all up to you.

Don't Be Sucked Dry.
Is there someone in your life who is emotionally draining you? You can't *always* say yes to need people like this! Next time you're approached by this person try saying that you're not available or limit the time you spend in conversation. Use the freed up time to connect with God in quiet or to be with someone that renews your soul and your faith. Being replenished and strengthening your boundary muscles will help you to be a cheerful giver.

Breath Prayer
You may feel anxious about the prospect of saying no to someone or having a difficult conversation, but don't let that stop you! Get into Jesus' easy yoke.

To help you "take courage" from Christ I invite you to do as I did before I dove into my ocean of fear: meditate on Paul's words in Philippians 4. He wrote these powerful, Spirit-inspired words when he was being persecuted in jail. For him being in jail meant being chained to a prison guard who was a boring, smelly, foul-mouthed, brute thug! And yet he says:

> Rejoice in the Lord always. I will say it again: Rejoice!... Do not be anxious about anything... If anything is excellent or praiseworthy—think about such things...

I have learned to be content whatever the circumstances. I know what it is to be in need, and I know what it is to have plenty. I have learned the secret of being content in any and every situation, whether well fed or hungry, whether living in plenty or in want. I can do everything through him who gives me strength (Philippians 4:4,6,8,11-13).

Paul wasn't defined by his visible circumstance of being chained to an ogre he was appreciating that he was in the wide-open spaces of the kingdom of the heavens! The peace of Christ was "guarding" his mind and heart (Philippians 4:7). Shielded by kingdom of God boundaries he wasn't anxious, resentful, or complaining about the injustice of his situation – he was in Jesus' easy yoke.

I invite you to cultivate Paul's reliance upon God's wonderful kingdom in his midst to help you deal with an enmeshed or stress-filled relationship with strong personal boundaries. We want to learn to let go of trying to control our relationship (which is to abandon outcomes to God as we learned earlier) and accept that things may be harmonious or they may be conflictual, but either way I trust the Sovereign Lord's rule in my life, knowing that because I love him and am seeking his will that he is working all things together for my good (Romans 8:28).

To build up your relational boundaries try using my Breath Prayer from Philippians 4:11-13: "In Christ I'm strong... in conflict or harmony." It's a simple way to pray the peace of God's kingdom deep into our hearts, letting it, rather than our stress, shape and form us.

You can use this Breath Prayer to watch and pray with Jesus by anticipating a conflict, guilt trip, or other stress on your boundaries in a particular relationship. Imagine yourself in the stressful relationship situation... Talk to your gracious Lord and Savior about how you feel... Now offer the Breath Prayer:

Breathe in to receive the Lord's blessing: "In Christ I'm strong…" Breathe out to let go, trusting the outcomes to the Sovereign Lord: "…in conflict or harmony."

Breathe in (trust) the reality of God's invisible kingdom all around you: "In Christ I'm strong…" Breathe out to refuse to be defined by your visible circumstances: "…in conflict or harmony."

You may find it better fits your particular need to change the wording of the Breath Prayer in one of these ways (or another way!):

"In Christ I'm strong… to help others or say no"

"In Christ I'm strong… when mistreated or loved"

"In Christ I'm strong… when praised or criticized"

"In Christ I'm strong… when alone or accepted"

Or, still staying with Paul's teaching in Philippians 4, you can substitute the word "content" for strong: "In Christ I'm content… in conflict or harmony."

Salty Questions

Sharing your heart and praying with a friend is an important part of how God helps you have the strength to set needed limits in your relationships. You and your friends need the encouragement that comes from checking in with one another on how you're doing with living in Jesus' easy yoke instead of anxiously walking on eggshells around people or pressuring yourself to fix their problems. These salty questions are designed to preserve learning, add God-flavor to life, and elicit thirst for more of God.

What are you learning about life in God's kingdom and setting boundaries in your relationships?

Do you enmesh with other people emotionally or do too much to help them? What is an example?

How did you do with setting boundaries this week and finding security and strength in Jesus' easy yoke?

You Can Live in Jesus' Easy Yoke: Lesson #8
Be God's Wildflower

A youth pastor named Justin was overstressed. He was trying so hard to be the ideal pastor to his high school students. He was doing a great job, but he didn't feel like it because he kept comparing himself to other pastors who he thought were more successful.

Whenever a student wasn't paying attention to his message or stopped attending he took it personally. He thought to himself, *I'm not as dynamic as other youth pastors. I need to make things more exciting so that more students will come. And I need to do a better job of developing leaders who assimilate new people.*

I asked Justin whose voice it was that was telling him he needed to be a better youth pastor.

"The Senior Pastor," he replied. "He's putting pressure on me to get more kids involved. And he's right our numbers aren't increasing."

"How about when you were growing up? Did anyone talk down to you?"

"Well, I was never able to be good enough for my father, but we didn't have much of a relationship. He divorced my mom when I was in high school and moved to another state. Even before then he wasn't around much and when he was home he was drinking.

"I remember when I was about seven or eight years old I kept asking him to play catch with me and finally one day we did. He actually bought me a glove and a ball – I was so excited! But I was having trouble learning to throw. He tried to teach me, but he got frustrated with me and I started crying. I did my best when threw him the ball, but I was awkward and my throws were bad. Finally he yelled, 'Justin, you throw like a girl! Why can you be like your older brother' and he walked away.

"That's what it was like. My grades weren't good enough because I didn't get A's like my little sister. And I didn't play sports or do anything as good as my brother."

All Justin wanted was his dad's approval. But he had almost no connection with him, except to hear about what he was doing wrong. He knew his father was wrong to be that way. Justin had forgiven him, but on a deeper level he couldn't get free of feeling like he had to excel in order to be acceptable. He felt like an average pastor and that felt bad. Until he was a *standout* pastor who was recognized for having a great ministry he couldn't relax.

I Felt Inadequate Too
I want to tell you about a time that like Justin I was feeling ordinary and inadequate.

I bet that sometimes you feel like you're not _____ enough. Not pretty enough. Not smart enough. Not wealthy enough. Not popular enough. Not accomplishing enough. Not holy enough.

You and I may fill in the blank differently, but we all want to be *enough*. And we may feel that to be enough we need to be ideal.

A number of years ago and Kristi and I were on a retreat with a group of Christian leaders. We were getting away for some days of teaching, community, and solitude. We practiced a variety of spiritual disciplines together and separately, all designed to help us to connect more intimately with Jesus so that we could become more like him in life and ministry.

Being quiet and still before God opened up my heart. I became painfully aware of some deep feelings that I was deficient. (Often when we slow down and get still to pray for an extended time we become aware of inner distress, which is why we tend to stay busy!) I felt that I was not doing enough with my life: I was not excelling in Christian ministry like some of my peers were. They were writing books and leading great classes and retreats. They were living out dreams similar to mine and they were being recognized by other people for their ministry.

But I didn't want to be jealous or competitive. These people were my friends and they were serving the Lord and helping others!

Make Yourself Stand Out
When we believe that we are not _____ enough we are not in the easy yoke of Jesus. Instead we become anxious or insecure. We're afraid to have our deficiencies exposed. We're under pressure to be better. We may be jealous or competitive toward those who seem to have the attractiveness or success that we want. Worried about our performance and ourselves we're not prepared to give the people we interact with the blessing from God that they need.

Commonly in our culture the way we deal with feeling that we're not enough is to make ourselves stand out. Probably you're familiar with some of these common "motivational" sayings. Maybe you've tried to live by one or more of these messages:

"You have to do (or look) better"

"You never get a second chance to make a first impression"

"Strive to be better than your competition"

"The will to win is everything"

"Climb to the top of the ladder"

"You're only as good as your last performance"

Are these messages good coaching? As you deal with challenges in your business, relationships, or ministry is God urging you to make yourself stand out?

Are You a Perfectionist?
Many people I talk with are like Justin and their character
has formed around a "make yourself stand out" narrative.
This leads to perfectionism, relying on your own abilities
and efforts to be more ideal in some area of your life.

You can take the following short survey to help you see to
what extent you may have perfectionistic tendencies. For
each question below answer "yes" if it's generally true of
you and "no" if it's generally *not* true of you.

- I often think that I should've done better than I did.
- I tend to put things off if I don't have the time to do
  them perfectly.
- I'm afraid to fail when working on an important
  project.
- I strive to impress others with my best qualities or
  accomplishments.
- I think less of myself if I repeat a mistake.
- I strive to maintain control of my emotions at all
  times.
- I get upset when things don't go as planned.
- I am often disappointed in the quality of other
  people's work.
- I feel that my standards couldn't be too high.
- I'm afraid that people will think less of me if I fail.
- I'm constantly trying to improve myself.
- I'm unhappy if anything I do is considered average.
- My home and office need to be clean and orderly
  always.
- I feel inferior to others who are more intelligent,
  attractive, or successful than I.
- I must look my very best whenever I'm out in
  public.

- If you have five or more yes answers to these questions it suggests that you struggle with perfectionism and are in great need of absorbing more of God's grace.

The Grace Antidote

The "You can do better! Make yourself stand out!" narrative that is so popular today in coaching, counseling, motivational talks, sermons, and self-help books is completely opposed to Jesus' Gospel, often in its content, always in its spirit.

Trying to be more ideal perpetuates perfectionism. It puts self on the throne of your heart rather than Christ and it leads to anxiety. It's a futile, anxiety-filled attempt to overcome feeling inadequate or deficient. No matter how good you look or how much you achieve or how much recognition and attention you get from people you will still feel empty and inadequate inside and the pressure to keep doing better will never go away. There will always be "more" and someone else who seems to have it that you'll be jealous of or competitive with.

When I became jealous and competitive of my friends that day on retreat I was being assaulted by this faulty thinking, "Make yourself stand out." The world, my flesh (natural abilities apart from God), and the devil were ganging up on me to take me out of the mind of Christ, the truths of Scripture that took on flesh and blood in Jesus Christ. Without realizing it I was turning away from Christ's smile and open arms and turning to myself; I was believing lies and half-truths that constantly buzz around in our airwaves.

Jesus Gospel is so counter-cultural, so wonderfully contrary to the world's way of trying to make ourselves stand out: "Think again about how you're living your life in view of your opportunity to do all that you do as my apprentice in God's Kingdom" (Matthew 4:17, paraphrase). This is a message of extravagant grace! Whoever you are, whatever you look like, whatever you've done or haven't done, whatever people say about you, take heart because you are loved and accepted for who you are.

What Good News! Anyone can live in God's Kingdom! Anyone can be with Jesus and become more like him! Anyone can live in Jesus' easy yoke! Anyone can thrive as a wildflower in the Father's field displaying God's color and beauty and sweet fragrance to passersby!

Jesus Resisted Competitiveness
The writer to Hebrews insists that Jesus, our sinless Lord and Savior, was tempted in all the ways that we are (Hebrews 4:15). So we know that Jesus was tempted to feel inadequate and jealous and to become competitive with others. Apparently we read about one such instance early in Jesus' ministry.

Before Jesus came on the public scene John the Baptist was recognized as the greatest prophet by all the people of Israel. People from all over Israel and beyond – men and women, the rich and the poor, the religious and the uneducated – journeyed into the desert to find John the Baptist and he would teach them to turn from their sins to the Lord and then he'd baptize them in the Jordan River to symbolize that God was cleansing them and giving them a fresh start.

Probably the high point of John's ministry was when Jesus Christ, the long-awaited Messiah and John's own cousin, came to him to be baptized, even though he had no sin to wash away. The Baptist was the forerunner leading up to Jesus and the one who was chosen by God to help Jesus to launch his public ministry!

But from that point forward Jesus' ministry grew and John's declined. John's best disciples left him to follow Jesus. Fewer and fewer people went to John to be baptized and more and more went to Jesus' followers. And people noticed this. In fact, they started keeping score! They saw that more people were going to Jesus rather than to John and they told John about this.

But John did not react with jealousy or competitive ambition – he didn't want to make himself stand out, he wanted to make Jesus stand out! So *he* uttered beautiful words about Jesus being the Bridegroom that belongs to the bride, the people of God, and that John himself was only the friend of the Bridegroom. His joy was to attend to the Bridegroom's needs, to wait for him and listen to him.[105] And he summarized his life purpose in perhaps the most humble and God-glorifying words of the whole Bible: "[Jesus] must become greater; I must become less" (John 3:30).

Now, let's turn to Jesus' part in this story. Have you ever noticed Jesus' reaction to the Pharisees making a contest out of how many people Jesus baptized and how many

---

[105] John 3:22-36 records this story.

John baptized? (Jesus himself did not offer water baptism to anyone, but he had his disciples do this.) "When the Lord learned of this, he left Judea and went back once more to Galilee" (John 4:3).

Jesus didn't want to compete with John – he wanted to bless him and his ministry! In fact, Jesus didn't even want to draw attention to his successes. When he performed miracles he often asked people to keep it secret. And when his popularity surged with the crowds he withdrew from them. Repeatedly, Jesus put the spotlight on the Father, saying the Father told him what to do and empowered him and that in everything he sought to glorify his name. In these ways Jesus practiced the discipline of secrecy.[106]

Jesus Became a Seed for Us

The Gospel of John tells a little-known story about Jesus resisting the temptation to compete as a public speaker.[107] Some God-fearing Greek men had came to Jerusalem to worship at the Passover Feast. They had heard about Jesus' great wisdom, compassion, and miracles and they used Philip, one of Jesus' disciples and a Greek, to get an interview with Jesus.

Especially in that day the Greeks were known for their ideas and philosophical discussions about life and religion. They wanted to meet the Jesus they heard about and

---

[106] Secrecy is the practice of doing your good deeds quietly, for God alone. See my article, "Secrecy," under "Spiritual Disciplines" at SoulShepherding.org.

[107] John 12:20-26.

question him. Perhaps the Greeks wanted Jesus to come and share his ideas with people in the great cities of the Roman world like Alexandria and Rome? This could be a great opportunity for Jesus to advance his career as a teacher and take his ideas to the world! He could show that his wisdom for life was better than other teachers – even that of Plato and Aristotle.

We know that the disciples and the people wanted Jesus to be Israel's Messiah-King in a political sense. They wanted Jesus to help them overthrow the Roman government and return the state of Israel to its glory years from when David was king. They would've been happy to accompany Jesus on a tour through the great cities of the Roman world so that Jesus could humble the Greek philosophers as he'd done repeatedly with the Jewish religious leaders. They could ride on the coattails of their brilliant teacher's expanding career! The disciples knew something about Jesus that most Christians today don't know: Jesus is the smartest person to ever live!

Jesus' answer to those who wanted him to help Israel overthrow Roman oppression or to advance his career as a public speaker was to tell a story:

There was a kernel of wheat that was clinging to its stalk. And it decided to let go – to stop clutching onto the life it knew and fall off the stalk, to the ground, and into the soil. It gave up life on its terms and let itself be buried in the earth. Then the rains came and the sun shined and where the seed had fallen a little seedling came up. And in time it grew to be a wheat plant with lots and lots of new seeds.

The seed had died. It gave up its life when it let go of the stalk. Not only did it die, but it disappeared. If you went to the spot where the seed fell and looked for it on the ground or under the surface of the ground you wouldn't find it. It was gone. The kernel of wheat gave up its life, let go of control, and received a new and abundant life.[108]

Jesus was saying: I am like that seed. I have given up my life. I have let go of this world. I'm not clinging to my rights and my privileges and my opportunities. I'm not using my power to establish Israel as the world superpower. And I'm not going to advance my career as a speaker. I've denied myself these things. I even let go of the privileges of my position in the Trinity in heaven and I took on human flesh to come to earth. I have denied myself many, many blessings of life on earth.

I'm not trying to make things happen for myself. I am submitted to the Father. I've given him charge of my life. And he has given me his life. He is producing from my life, many, many new seeds of life. And now I'm about to go to the Cross to be crucified to save you from your sins – and to show you how to let go of life on your terms and give it away to God.

The Apostle Paul Renounced Selfish Ambition

Tradition has passed onto us a picture of the Apostle Paul as a short man. In fact, Paul means "small." Perhaps like many other men he tried to compensate for being short. Whatever the reason, we know that Paul was an ambitious man with a superlative pedigree and list of achievements.

---

[108] My paraphrase of John 12:24.

He was perhaps the greatest and most accomplished Pharisee of his day. He was top dog in the religious world, which in that culture received the highest respect. But after he saw the Light of Christ on the Damascus Road and was converted he brought all of his ambition to the cross.

Paul had been a wild horse and he knew that he needed the Lord to corral and tame him. He had been ambitious, arrogant, jealous, and competitive. So he took off his religious image like a cloak and he discarded all the heavy responsibilities he was carrying. He made himself nothing and went off into the Arabian Desert in silence and solitude with the risen Christ for three years (Galatians 1:15-18). He became *passionately indifferent to all things except Christ.* O yes, dear Lord, may we, like your Apostle, be passionately indifferent to everything except you!

But whatever was to my profit I now consider loss for the sake of Christ. What is more, I consider everything a loss compared to the surpassing greatness of knowing Christ Jesus my Lord, for whose sake I have lost all things. I consider them rubbish, that I may gain Christ and be found in him, not having a righteousness of my own that comes from the law, but that which is through faith in Christ—the righteousness that comes from God and is by faith. I want to know Christ and the power of his resurrection and the fellowship of sharing in his sufferings, becoming like him in his death, and so, somehow, to attain to the resurrection from the dead.

Not that I have already obtained all this, or have already been made perfect, but I press on to take hold of that for which Christ Jesus took hold of me. Brothers, I do not consider myself yet to have taken hold of it. But one thing I do: Forgetting what is behind and straining toward what is ahead, I press on toward the goal to win the prize for which God has called me heavenward in Christ Jesus (Philippians 3:7-14).

The Humility of Christ

Paul became the humblest, most generous, most Christ-like disciple. And he is an especially helpful role model for us because his discipleship to Jesus was just like ours: he didn't have the advantage of physically living with and ministering side-by-side with Jesus, but was limited to relating with the risen Christ, invisible to the physical eye and present only to the eye of faith. Through the testimony of the Gospel writers and other Apostles, his years of quiet prayer in the desert, and practicing other spiritual disciplines, Paul learned to live his whole life with and for Jesus Christ.

Paul writes in words taught him by the Spirit of Christ and urges us to join him and take our selfish ambition and jealousy into the way of Christ's cross:

If you have any encouragement from being united with Christ, if any comfort from his love, if any fellowship with the Spirit, if any tenderness and compassion, then make my joy complete by being like-minded, having the same love, being one in spirit and purpose. Do nothing out of selfish ambition or vain conceit, but in humility consider others better than yourselves. Each of you should look not only to your own interests, but also to the interests of others.

Your attitude should be the same as that of Christ Jesus:
Who, being in very nature God,
did not consider equality with God something to be
grasped,
but made himself nothing,
taking the very nature of a servant,
being made in human likeness.
And being found in appearance as a man,
he humbled himself
and became obedient to death—
even death on a cross!
Therefore God exalted him to the highest place
and gave him the name that is above every name,
that at the name of Jesus every knee should bow,
in heaven and on earth and under the earth,
and every tongue confess that Jesus Christ is Lord,
to the glory of God the Father (Philippians 2:1-11).

God Showed me a Wildflower

A turning point for me to overcome feeling inadequate
and to leave jealousy and selfish ambition behind came
one day when I was walking and I was pouring out my
heart to Jesus. He began showing me what a glorious
scene He had created for me to be in with Him: the sun
was shining on us, the birds were singing over us, and we
were walking along a path that cut through a valley filled
with wildflowers.

I felt impressed to stop and *really look* at all the
wildflowers in front of me. There were so many! They
were so colorful! And they were just there because God
wanted them there. No person had planted them. God
sent breezes and birds to scatter seeds and he sent rain
and sun and grew the flowers. Thousands of people drove

by this valley every day just a block or two from where I was standing and yet very few of them ever walked over to appreciate these flowers.

Then God showed me a single wildflower surrounded by thousands of other flowers. I sensed him whisper to my heart words that spoke his life to me and renewed my soul. I believe his words are for you too...

Be like that flower before me. See how beautiful it is? See how happy it is? And yet it is lost in a sea of color and fragrance.

No one has ever laid eyes on that flower alone – those who stand where you are might see the whole field of wildflowers, but not this particular one. You say that this flower does not stand out, that it's not special. But *I appreciate this flower!* It is beautiful to me! And it is joining with all the other flowers in this valley to communicate my goodness and love to passersby.

I often thank God for that Christ-like wildflower and I remind myself to bloom where I am planted for God – even if no one else seems to notice. And I hold my head high and smile!

God's Wildflower
> My precious wildflower – smile!
> I have clothed you in heaven's splendor.
> Though you're lost to all in a field of blooms,
> You're seen by me and my sweet society.
> Don't worry about who sees your beauty
> Or about how much time you have to bloom.
> Be dead to the world and alive to me

For I planted you here and I know your name.

I am your Father smiling over you!
You're growing in the grace of my Sonlight,
Nourished by the rains from my mouth.
My choirs of angels, birds, and saints
Join me in singing my love song over you;
We delight to dance with you in Spirit breezes.
What joy it brings to us all in my kingdom
When you smile and sing back to me!

The Wildflower in the Bible
Later I saw the same wildflower in Psalm 103:15-17, which
I paraphrased this way:

I am God's Flower
As for me, my days are like grass,
I flourish like a wildflower in the Father's field,
Given life and color by the Son;
The Spirit blows over me and I am gone to heaven,
And my place remembers me no more.
But from everlasting to everlasting
The Lord's love is with me, as I revere him,
And his righteousness is with my children's
children.

Probably the Psalmist's words inspired Jesus when he said:
"See how the lilies of the field grow? Your Father clothes
them in splendor. So much more than this he clothes you
and loves you!" (Matthew 6:28-30, paraphrase). These
words from the Bible by David and Jesus helped me to
know that indeed God was the one speaking to me when I
saw that single wildflower in a field of thousands!

God's words are always blossoming if only we will stop, look, and smell their fragrance! It is only because of the living Word of God – the holy words revealed in the Bible, the voice that is continually speaking in thoughts and impressions, the Word made flesh in Jesus Christ – that we can continue to "live and move and have our being" (Acts 17:28).

God creates and sustains all life through his words (Psalm 19, Hebrews 4:12, 1 Peter 1:23). God's communications are not just true, they are real; they are *reality.* God's voice to us is like the manna that fell from heaven in the desert wilderness and the Israelites ate it and lived off of it for forty years (Exodus 16:4, Psalm 78:24). And God used the picture of me as his little flower to nourish my soul – and many other people who have told me how much this has ministered to them.

The Lord has Especially Chosen You!
Jeanne Guyon (1648-1717) was a French mystic who was persecuted by the religious authorities of the Catholic Church for her writings that empowered simple people to go directly to God through praying the Scriptures from their hearts. *Take Heart!* She has helped countless ordinary people live in the Father's field as glorious wildflowers![109]

---

[109] Jeanne Guyon's book, *A Short and Very Easy Method of Prayer* (later re-named *Experiencing the Depths of Jesus Christ)* evoked immediate controversy in the Catholic Church: stirring many in France to greater devotion to Christ, but leading to persecution and book burnings by the religious authorities of her day. Her book has become one of the most widely read devotional books of all time and had profound influence on many great Christian leaders including John

I give you an invitation: If you are thirsty, come to the living waters. Do not waste your precious time digging wells that have no water in them. If you are starving and can find nothing to satisfy your hunger, then come. Come, and you will be filled."

You who are poor, come.

You who are afflicted, come...

> Dear child of God, your Father has His arms of love open wide to you. Throw yourself into His arms. You who have strayed and wandered away as sheep, return to your Shepherd...

I especially address those of you who are very simple and you who are uneducated... You may think yourself the one farthest from a deep experience with the Lord; but, in fact, the Lord has *especially* chosen you! You are the one *most* suited to know Him well...

So let no one feel left out. Jesus Christ has called us all.

Oh, I suppose there is one group who *is* left out!
> Do not come if you have no heart. You see, before you come, there is one thing you must do: You must first give your heart to the Lord...

Wesley. Her words inspire beginners and the mature alike to devote themselves to Christ.

Once you have enjoyed your Lord and tasted the sweetness of His love [through praying the Scriptures and beholding Christ], you will find that even your selfish desires no longer hold any power. You will find it impossible to have pleasure in anything except Him...

I realize that some of you may feel that you are very slow, that you have a poor understanding, and that you are very unspiritual. Dear reader, there is nothing in this universe that is easier to obtain than the enjoyment of Jesus Christ! Your Lord is more present to you than you are to yourself! Furthermore, His desire to give Himself to you is *greater* than *your* desire to lay hold of Him.[110]

Be Immersed in Jesus' Reality
God is saying the same thing to us through Jeanne Guyon as the little wildflower: "You are significant to me! You are beautiful to me! Just be who I made you to be and let me love you. Stand tall and smile where I've placed you. Don't worry about who notices you. Just let your light shine for me."

This is the message of God's grace that helped Justin begin to experience healing from his perfectionism. He had to trust his heavenly Father at a deeper level and let go of his earthly father's rejections. He "knew" that the message of God's grace was throughout the Bible – he preached sermons on it! – but he didn't *know* it deep in his heart, he hadn't really trusted and relied on God's favor and unconditional love for him personally. He had to learn to live in Jesus' easy yoke of peace.

---

[110] Jeanne Guyon, *Experiencing the Depths of Jesus Christ* by Jeanne Guyon (1685) p. 2-4.

To be yoked to Jesus as his apprentice is to join him in his baptism,[111] not only as a sacrament of water baptism, but also as a *continuous immersion in the reality of the kingdom of the heavens that baptism initiates us into.* To be baptized means more than getting wet while a pastor says, "I baptize you in the name of the Father, the Son, and the Spirit." Names in the Bible reflect the *reality* behind them. *To be baptized is to be submerged in the Trinitarian presence.*[112]

The real waters of baptism are the living waters of God's Spirit, God's presence and power right now as we're doing whatever we're doing. Immersing ourselves in a consciousness of the Trinitarian reality washes and renews us. And redefines our identity over time – forming us in the glorious image of Christ. We need this healing and renewal!

Jesus' baptism shows us a picture of the life that God has for us. His baptism is a Theophany, a manifestation of the Trinity.[113] And it's an opportunity for us in meditation and prayer to remind ourselves that right now, wherever we are, through trusting in Christ, we can appreciate that we

---

[111] Mark 1:1-15 tells the story of Jesus' baptism.

[112] This is how Dallas Willard paraphrases Jesus words about baptism in Matthew 28:18-20.

[113] An example of a Theophany in the Bible is the Lord appearing to Abraham in the three angelic visitors that represented the Trinity (Genesis 18:1-10).

are immersed in the loving presence of the Father, Son, and Spirit.

Imagine Yourself Baptized in Christ
Oh, to be free to be our true self, created and re-created by the Lord, immersed in God's love for us through Christ!

See Jesus with John the Baptist, standing in the Jordan River...

See the Holy Spirit in the form of a dove descending from the skies and landing on Jesus, remaining on his shoulder...

Hear the Father God's voice roll like thunder, powerful and deep, as he publicly affirms Jesus: "This is my beloved Son and in him I am well pleased."

See yourself baptized, submerged not only in the water, but in the Trinitarian reality...

Be washed... Be renewed... Be embraced in the love of God...

As you come up the Holy Spirit lands on *you* as a dove and he remains on *you*...

Listen: the Father is speaking to you and he wants everyone to hear: *"You* are my beloved son/daughter. In you I am well pleased..."

When we live in the Trinitarian reality, which is the kingdom of God and the grace of Christ, then we will be free of anxiety, jealousy, and competiveness. We'll be ready to bless and encourage others, even those who are difficult or who offend us because we're living in a different world than the one we see – it's a world in which, "God demonstrates his own love for us in this: While we were still sinners, Christ died for us" (Romans 5:8) and "We love because [God] first loved us" (1 John 4:19).

Spiritual Exercise: Bless your Competitors

Jesus taught us, "Bless those that curse you" (Luke 6:28). Jesus is teaching us to share God's mercy and grace not only with people who utter a curse against us or swear at us but also for anyone who offends us or distresses us in some way. A common stress that comes up in our relationships, including with our loved ones, friends, neighbors, and co-workers is to be tempted to become jealous or competitive.

Justin felt jealous and amped up his perfectionism when he saw a dynamic youth pastor with a growing ministry. Maybe you're tempted to compare yourself when you see someone who has a new outfit or a new car, is getting lots of attention, has money, or is successful. Probably most every day you run into a "competitor" who either passes you on the road, cuts in front of you in line, receives credit that you deserve, gets a deal that you worked for, or re-directs a conversation away from you to him or herself. How do you react when someone has what you wish you had? Maybe you feel inadequate or jealous? Maybe you become competitive and try to do better or get ahead?

Those who live in the easy yoke of Jesus are able and prepared to bless difficult people – easily and naturally, without pressure or condemnation and without being a doormat or not having any boundaries. It's a matter of growing in God's grace and overflowing with his blessings.

Identify someone who is like a competitor to you. In prayer talk to the Lord about how you feel about this situation...

Don't guilt trip yourself for having negative thoughts or emotions! Don't pressure yourself to try harder to do good! Instead, purpose to keep training with Jesus to live in his easy yoke and become a *different kind of person,* someone who is prepared to bless other people, including your competition.

Ask God to help you to think of a way that you can bless your competitor *secretly,* without telling anyone what you're doing and why! (Except you may find it important to tell your spiritual growth partner or group about this for your continued learning and to encourage them.)

This can be as simple as letting people cut in front of you on the road or in line. Or try blessing the competitor you identified by giving away a business referral, sending an encouragement card or note, or offering prayers.

Breath Prayer
Recall Paul's words in Philippians 2:3 about Christ's "kenosis" or self-emptying love: "Do nothing out of selfish ambition or vain conceit, but in humility consider others better than yourselves."

You can use these words to pray for someone that you're jealous of or feel competitive with. Or pray them for someone who has mistreated you. But don't make the mistake of misusing Paul's words to heap onto yourself guilt and pressure! Paul is *not* saying, "You shouldn't feel jealous or ambitious. And shame on you if you do!" He is *not* saying, "You don't matter. Don't pay attention to your own needs just treat other people with love and respect."

The point here is that Jesus, the Lord Almighty and King of kings, the Son of God, in his incarnation picked up a towel, got on his knees, and washed our dirty feet! (John 13:1-17). He serves us even though we don't deserve it. If we appreciate the gift of his generous kindness to us then we'll learn to share it with others: we will bless and serve others as he does for us.

You might try praying Philippians 2:3 as a Breath Prayer like this: "In Christ's humility... consider others more than yourself."

Breathe in to receive as you think: "In Christ's humility..."

Breathe out to share as you think: "Consider others more than yourself."

Perhaps it'd help you to go farther in using your body by getting on your knees and/or using your hands to engage your mind and express your prayer...

Kneel before the Lord quietly. Deliberately wait to breathe for a while, feeling your longing for oxygen. As you wait raise your hands in quiet prayer, waiting to breathe, hands raised high in worship of the Lord who humbly serves you...

Then slowly breathe in the words, "In Christ's humility" as you pull your hands toward your chest, receiving Christ's generous, gracious, servant love...

Then exhale the words, "Consider others better than yourself" as you extend your hands outward, overflowing with Christ's consideration and esteem for others.

Practice whatever prayer rhythm helps you. Then focus your praying on blessing someone in particular that you might be tempted to compete with...

Salty Questions
Feeling like we're not _____ enough and then being alone with that stress or hurt is what makes us susceptible to have selfish ambition or envy in our relationships. This emphasizes the importance of paying close attention to our personal and spiritual experiences and then sharing honestly with our friend or group. As we do this it helps us to draw closer to Christ in one another:

What do wildflowers tell you about Jesus' easy yoke?

What is an example of you feeling inadequate, jealous, or competitive recently?

Did you offer words of blessing or a secret prayer for a competitor this week? How did it affect you?

CPSIA information can be obtained at www.ICGtesting.com
Printed in the USA
LVOW101848240912

300100LV00012B/57/P